C000271451

Conscious Cooking

Cook Well, Eat Well, Live Well

Published by The Body Retreat

Copyright © 2016 by Juls Abernethy

The content of this book is for general instruction only. Each person's physical and emotional condition is unique. The instruction in this book is not intended to replace or interrupt the reader's relationship with a physician or other professional. Please consult your doctor for matters pertaining to your specific health and diet.

All rights reserved. No part of this publication may be reproduced, distributed, or transmitted in any form or by any means, including photocopying, recording, or other electronic or mechanical methods, without the prior written permission of the publisher or author, except in the case of brief quotations embodied in critical reviews and certain other noncommercial uses permitted by copyright law. For permission requests, e-mail the publisher or author at Juls@ thebodyretreat.co.uk

To contact the publisher, visit www.thebodyretreat.co.uk

To contact the author, visit www.thebodyretreat.co.uk

Photographer: Annie Armitage

Editor: Jane Alexander

ISBN-13: 978-0995531307

Dedication

For J, K & E for keeping me sane through this process

I'd like to thank Carolyn Palmer for her unwavering patience and support in the early days of the book process, thank you for helping me to take some very raw material and begin the process of creating a cookery book. A big thank you to Jane Alexander for her wonderful editing skills, I wish I had you beside me every time time I press send on any written work. Thank you to Kate Delmar Morgan who works with us at The Body Retreat, working with the best means that I have to keep learning to keep up and I have learnt such a lot from you. Finally a HUGE THANK YOU to all the gorgeous and supportive women who have joined us at The Body Retreat, your kind words about the food, your feedback on recipes, your continuously keeping me accountable for the book not to mention your patience as you all waited and waited for the book to arrive, I feel very lucky to have had such generous support.

 Copyright © 2016 Conscious Cooking

Copyright © 2016 Conscious Cooking

Copyright © 2016 Conscious Cooking

FOREWORD FOR CONSCIOUS COOKING

If you are looking for a tool to help you transform your current dietary habits into a new, lifelong, set of more healthful ones then this is the book for you.

I am honoured to be writing a Foreword for this wonderful recipe book by Juls Abernethy. I call it a recipe book but actually it is much more than that. It is more of a strategy to encourage you to make a personal change in how you approach food and eating for the rest of your life. It contains some fundamental nutrition information that is easy to understand, achievable lifestyle tips plus some wonderful recipes that are nutritious not to mention tasty.

I am a Registered Nutritional Therapist based in South West London and after studying Nutrition for four years I began practising, working with many individuals to help them improve their health by improving the food choices they make. I have now been practising for over ten years and have worked with a large number of clients with a huge variety of health issues. The kind of information and advice that I provide can make a life changing impact to an individual. However, it is one thing to advise someone on how to improve their food intake to support their health and help improve their symptoms in a consultation room, but it is another thing entirely to instigate behaviour change. This can be a big issue for some clients and therefore they can really struggle. They can become disillusioned and this in turn can prevent them from achieving their goals. The key to making changes is to set realistic goals and achieve them and this book can really help. It will challenge your current thinking and provide you the means to make a paradigm shift.

I have known Juls for over five years and she has always been an accomplished cook but she has now also developed into a wonderful healthy chef. She has a tremendous interest in the field of nutrition and attends regular professional courses on various nutrition topics. She has also travelled her own dietary journey and she talks about that here in her book. She knows full well the struggles that a journey of change might take. I deliver the Nutrition Workshops for The Body Retreat and I know that what I say in those workshops is fully supported by Jul's cooking and her ethos.

I have had the pleasure of trying a number of the dishes included in this book and do not only give them my professional 'seal of approval' for their nutritional excellence but they are incredibly tasty too! She makes the recipes and methods as easy as possible to prepare without losing the essence of the dish. Juls perfects the dishes with magnificent nutritionally dense ingredients providing all manner of health benefits. These recipes have the potential to become part of your everyday routine for the future. Many of these dishes can be prepared at home and taken to your workplace to enhance your nutrition and performance throughout the day. There are meals that are great for one person, two people or larger families plus those that can be quickly prepared for when friends are over for lunch or dinner.

I am delighted that Juls is giving so many more people the opportunity to experience her recipes. She has truly managed the challenging art of transferring her creative chef and nutrition thoughts to paper. Her dishes are full of integrity, fresh and nutritious ingredients and I for one can't wait to indulge!

Kate Delmar-Morgan
Registered Nutritional Therapist
BSc Hons, mBANT, rCNHC

 Copyright © 2016 Concious Cooking

Conscious
COOKING

INTRODUCTION

THIS IS NOT A DIET BOOK

This book is not fat-free, sugar-free, carb-free: no way!

The one thing it is, is fad free.

Conscious Cooking is a brand new way of getting both a great body and a great life, eating real food.

The Conscious Cooking approach is very different from "dieting". Here at the Body Retreat we're all about learning to listen to our bodies, about forming a better relationship with food. We believe in long term solutions to eating issues rather than quick, temporary fixes.

Every time you practice Conscious Cooking you are making a step in the right direction. Each step you take will coax you into sensible eating behaviour which will, ultimately, let you reach a healthy weight – and stay at that healthy weight, not just for a few days, weeks or months – but for always. Yes, you read that right – we can help you lose weight (if you need to) and keep it off for good and all.

Conscious Cooking is about making healthy conscious choices when you are shopping, planning and preparing meals. It's not only about what to eat for optimum health but how and when to eat it.

    Copyright © 2016 Conscious Cooking

It's not about excluding foods, it really isn't. In fact we will only ask you to consider excluding two types of food:

1. Anything processed. If the ingredients read like a chemistry paper, do not eat it.
2. Artificial sweeteners. The body does not distinguish between sugar and sweeteners so you may be causing damage to your system, not to mention links to cancer and other chronic diseases. Truly, it's not worth it.

So, yes, we're asking you – where possible – to cook from scratch, to make your own meals (or to choose very carefully when eating out or buying a take-away). Don't panic! You don't have to become a gourmet chef or to spend hours slaving over a hot stove. Conscious Cooking is mostly about fast cooking. The vast majority of the recipes in this book take only minutes to prepare and present. Other are quick to prepare but then you can just pop them in the oven or in a slow cooker for hassle-free comfort food.

Truly, they are simplicity itself.

All our Body Retreat guests leave with printed recipe sheets but we're constantly being asked for all the information we give out to be put together in one place. Hence this book. We hope you enjoy it.

 Copyright © 2016 Conscious Cooking

I'm Juls Abernethy, a hypnotherapist and NLP trainer with a special interest in women's wellbeing, weight management, stress and sleep. My other great passion is food and nutrition, and I am responsible for all the food on our retreats. My co-founder, Julie Brealy, is in charge of the exercise part of the Body Retreat equation, so you won't hear her voice so much in this book (but that doesn't mean you should shirk the exercise!).

We started The Body Retreat back in 2011 and, since then, we have empowered hundreds of women to reclaim control of their health and fitness. Our retreats aren't just about shedding pounds (though they do that, very effectively), they're all about helping women define themselves on their own terms. We don't believe any woman should be dictated to by society or scales. We want you to leave feeling a greater sense of wellbeing – one that stays with you long-term, not just for a few days post-retreat.

We have helped loads of women turn their backs on decades of dodgy dieting so they can finally achieve the body and fitness they want, and regain the energy and zest for life we all deserve.

Many women join us as they realise that something has to change with their current

About US

lifestyle but they are not sure what to do or how to begin.

At The Body Retreat we want to help you respect and protect your body for life.
Our various programmes have been put together lovingly and mindfully and combine evidence-based research with our own practical and professional experience. They are all inspiring (and good fun) and guaranteed to produce results.

Far from being a quick fix, our retreats are designed to help you find balance in the long term by focusing holistically on four pillars of wellbeing – Behaviour, Nutrition, Exercise and – possibly the best bit – Rest & Relaxation. This approach was revolutionary when we started and is at the forefront of all our events.

 Copyright © 2016 Conscious Cooking

My Food
JOURNEY

Let me tell you about my food background. I (Juls) was raised by my Irish grandmother in the frugal 1970s. Being a fussy eater was simply never an option.

Cheaper cuts of meat, seasonal veggies and of course the humble potato played a huge part of my childhood plate. I was brought up on simple, healthy hearty food. Of course my grandmother was cooking consciously, without calling it that - almost everything we ate was sourced locally, in season and then cooked simply.

One pot wonders were big in our house and they are still big in my house today. I love how quick, convenient they are and very importantly how they save on the washing up.

When I left Ireland to go to University to study Hotel and Catering Management the world of fine dining was opened up to me. Stints working in some of the UK's best hotels gave me a glimpse of how exquisite food could be.

When I made the decision to take on the cooking at The Body Retreat, I went back to college to refresh my skills, choosing

Ashburton Cookery School in Devon, where Michelin starred chefs taught me how to make fresh, local and often humble ingredients sing.

I was hooked.

I have now studied the science of Nutrition and Fat Loss. I have also trained in psychotherapy and hypnotherapy – so I understand how the mind and emotions have as much to do with weight loss and health as do nutrients and calorie intake. Our experience of years at The Body Retreat, working with a huge number of women, all different ages, all with different issues, has expanded and refined my knowledge. At The Body Retreat we create meal plans and dishes that are healthy, nutritious and, above all, totally delicious. I'm still a big foodie and love trying new places to eat, new recipes and, best of all, playing with new ingredients.

These dishes reflect our ethos at The Body Retreat – they are warm, down to earth dishes that are all about the produce, the cook and the eater.

Ditch The Diet –
GET CONSCIOUS!

Diets make you unhappy, they remind you of all the things you cannot and 'should not' eat.

But we are creatures of desire and we naturally move towards the things we want. Tell us we can't have this or that and we're setting ourselves up for rebellion – the subconscious will kick back and sabotage you pretty much each and every time.

Diets are all about deprivation. At the Body Retreat we believe food should be about joy and pleasure. Diets take away your power, turning you into a food slave. We believe you should be the one in control; the one who chooses what to eat and what not to eat.

Many diets are also nutritionally imbalanced and far too limited in their food choices. I have a real concern that some diet fads leave people open to developing nutritional deficiencies, to gaining food intolerances, and even to encouraging eating disorders.

Something else we see time and again with women who come on our retreats is the yo-yo effect. You can stick to a strict diet for a certain amount of time and, yes, lose weight but then, at some point, you will kick back and the pendulum will swing back the other way. The weight will pile back on. That really is bad for your health, not to mention your morale

Why Conscious COOKING?

Conscious Cooking is the opposite of dieting – it gives you freedom and choice – you get to decide exactly how you will feed your mind and body. Does that sound scary? Licence to eat everything and anything? No. Conscious Cooking is about delicious and nutritious food that never makes you feel deprived or miserable.

A healthy lifestyle includes good, real food; food that sustains life; that gives your body energy and your mind focus; food that makes your spirit soar. Just because you can eat a takeaway doesn't mean you have to. Why accept the sluggish feeling of eating lots of junk food or nutritionally empty foods? Once you start eating consciously, you will start making choices that really support your body and your life. You will start eating real food in reasonable amounts. What is reasonable? That entirely depends on the day and your activity levels, your mood, your cycle and your location. But we will look at that in more detail later in the book.

Doubtless you have already tried fat-free, sugar-free and carb-free regimes. I expect you've fasted and juiced every which way. No doubt you've counted every calorie and tried all manner of clubs, classes, shakes and supplements? Really, is there any end to the number of diet fads out there? Well this is FAD FREE cooking and eating for life.

This is not about abstinence and denial – no way! This is all about choice. This is about your conscious choice to eat in a way that respects and protects your body.

This book provides you with a wide range of every day recipes that you can relax and enjoy in the firm knowledge that they are quietly, calmly, effectively contributing to your good health.

I make you a firm promise that, while they are good for you, they aren't remotely hair-shirt rabbit food. This is real, gutsy tasty food. I also promise, hand on heart, that the recipes are easy to follow and the ingredients easy to find. There's nothing worse than going to make a recipe and finding that half the ingredients are only available from specialist stores or via mail order. This is real food for real people. This is the food I cook in my kitchen and on our retreats. I love cooking and I love good food, but I'm not about spending half my life fiddling around over the stove.

 Copyright © 2016 Conscious Cooking

The how, when and what of
EATING

The big difference in this book is that we won't just talk about what you should eat but give you guidelines on how and when to eat it too. What most healthy eating books miss out on is the psychology of food and also the physiology of eating. I have a firm grounding in both psychology and nutrition – I know what bodies need and what minds like to do to scupper bodies getting what they need. But, rest assured, I have worked out ways to get your mind onside, making it easier to pick healthy choices, day in, day out.

Let me re-iterate, this is not a diet cookbook. Diets promise so much and yet most deliver so little.

No matter how determined you are at the beginning, the restriction that dieting imposes on you makes it impossible to stick to long term. This book really is different. Honestly, it is. This is all about adopting a new way of eating for life.

Before we launch into the recipes, I'd just like to go over some points that will help you achieve the results you want. I know it's tempting to head straight for the recipes but do please read through the guidelines for good eating first. I have kept them simple but understanding how and when you should eat, as well as what you should eat, is really vital.

LET'S GET STARTED!

 Copyright © 2016 Conscious Cooking

General GUIDELINES

This is primarily a recipe book so I don't want to inundate you with masses of theory, but there are some principles and guidelines which will really help you shift your diet – and your whole life. So let's just quickly run over some of the principles we teach at our retreats.

THE EIGHT BASIC PRINCIPLES FOR GOOD EATING & GOOD HEALTH

When it comes to eating for health it's not just about what you eat, but also about how and when you eat. Making small subtle changes to how and when you eat means that you get the maximum nutritional value and the maximum natural energy from the foods you have chosen. These are the eight principles that will make all the difference.

These are the eight principles that will make all the difference.

1. **Eat when you are hungry.** By this I mean when you are truly hungry, as in body hungry not mind hungry. So beware if you feel hungry when really you're feeling bored, or stressed or unhappy. Equally check that you are hungry, not thirsty. Often our bodies can't differentiate between the two – so try drinking a glass of water before you reach for that snack.

2. **Eat sitting down in a calm environment.** Ideally this should be at a table. So, you won't be eating in the car, on the train, at your desk with the phone ringing and your PC glaring. And you won't be eating walking down the road, or standing in the kitchen.

3. **Eat without distractions.** Distractions include television, newspaper, books, intense or anxiety producing conversation. In an ideal world you would eat in silence, focusing only on your food. Be careful of music. It has been long proven that we eat to the beat. Fast food restaurants blast out fast poppy music as they want you in and out quickly. By contrast fine dining restaurants play slow relaxing music as they want you to stay and spend.

 Copyright © 2016 Conscious Cooking

4. **Eat only what your body wants and needs.** Note – this is probably a big difference from what your mind wants!

5. **Eat until you are satisfied.** Note – this is very different from full up or stuffed to the gills.

   Remind yourself: If I continue eating when I am no longer hungry it is the same thing as throwing it away. It is better to throw it in the rubbish bin or on the compost heap rather than make your belly the bin!

6. **Eat in full view of others (or as if you were).** What does this mean? Basically it's about no secret eating; no hiding in a corner scarfing down a bag of sweets or a packet of biscuits. Eating should not be a shameful thing.

7. **Eat with enjoyment and pleasure.** Savour each and every mouthful. Follow the Conscious Eating Practice we'll discuss next to make sure all your eating is mindful.

8. **Eat using the 80/20 principle.** This is very simple. Providing you eat clean, healthy delicious food for 80 percent of the time, you can eat whatever you like for the remaining 20 percent. How you choose to do that is entirely up to you. Some people have a small daily indulgence; others prefer to eat 'clean' for six days of the week and have whatever they fancy on the seventh day. Or maybe 80 percent of the time you choose seasonal produce and for 20 percent you choose exotic world produce. Adopting the 80/20 principle means that you are always in balance, never deprived, never restricted but free to make choices that suit your lifestyle and budgets.

    Copyright © 2016 Conscious Cooking

Keep it
SIMPLE

So you think you don't have time for good food? Wrong. This collection of recipes has everything from two minute snacks to a 90 second breakfast (yes, seriously). Okay, so there's a curry that takes 40 minutes to cook but, here's the key, it takes next to no time to prepare.

We do not need to over-complicate food. Ten to one, you already know what areas of your diet could be cleaned up. Are you a lazy eater stocking up on processed foods and takeaways? Maybe you're a portion distorter who eats "healthy foods" but just too much of them? Or a comfort eater who eats to change how they feel and tends to eat high sugar, high fat meals and snacks.

Conscious Cooking works to improve your health and wellbeing through three simple concepts:
• Quality
• Consistency
• Choice

Conscious Cooking leads to eating good food which in turn makes you feel and look good. Conscious Cooking is about making healthy choices that work for you.

Choice means that you can take control.

Choice means that you enjoy flexibility.

Choice means freedom.

But choice also means responsibility.

Think about that word for a moment. Responsibility. It means making a response based on your ability at that time.

It is really about making the right choice that works for you right now.

How do you know if it is the right choice? Well, all the great thinkers tell us that when it comes to choosing, the answer is "keep it simple".

Good shopping is 70 percent of any good recipe. Buy the best quality ingredients that you can afford, treat them simply and cook them quickly and you cannot go wrong.

 Copyright © 2016 Conscious Cooking

Seasonal EATING

We firmly believe that we should buy our food locally and seasonally where possible and practical. Does that mean there is no banana or pineapple on our retreats or in this book? No, of course not. But I do want you to think about the provenance of your food.

I just love the seasonality of produce. I have learnt to wean myself off the "I want everything NOW" convenience style shopping and eating of the 21st century. Now I advocate the 80/20 rule when it comes to choosing produce. So 80 percent of the time I choose local, seasonal British produce and for the remaining 20 percent I let myself go wild and treat myself to pineapple, mango and other exotics.

By eating seasonally you learn to enjoy foods when they are at their best, rather than eating anaemic, often tasteless versions that have been flown in while still unripe or forced in hothouses, plastered with pesticides. Why eat flaccid foreign strawberries in winter when you could enjoy the sweet ripeness of local strawberries in May/June? I long for signs of asparagus and rhubarb, my most favourite fruits. Both are eaten with relish and real delight because they are only with us for a few short months.

80/20 helps you through those winter months when fresh veggies and fruits are limited and I am also a sucker for occasional tropical fruit salad too. Check out our fruit and seed salad.

Make a conscious effort to find the best, local and seasonal produce.

Supermarkets label fruit and vegetables with the country of origin – look to eat first British, then European and then the Rest of the World. Eating home grown and seasonally available produce means that food is fresher; it has had to travel less far. Check out farmers' markets, farm shops and organic box delivery systems – these are a great convenient way to shop seasonally.

 Copyright © 2016 Conscious Cooking

Making conscious choices every day means that you can tip the balance in favour of increasing your health and wellness. Each small conscious choice you make each day takes you one step closer to creating healthy habits for life.

In an ideal world, of course, your entire diet would be organic. Food grown without pesticides, fungicides, hormones and other chemicals are naturally better for our health and for the health of the planet. However I'm a realist. Organic food is expensive and not always available. There are, nonetheless, occasions where I would beg you to think carefully. A couple of "no brainers" as far as both optimum health and good conscious (eating) go – all meat and dairy should be organic and free range. At The Body Retreat we are big believers in only eating happy animals – ones whom have been treated with respect.

When it comes to fish – likewise – we try where possible to use sustainable fish sources. Check out www.msc.org.

 Copyright © 2016 Conscious Cooking

BREAKFAST

Your Daily Diet

Let's run through how your daily diet should look. All too often people can't lose weight because they simply aren't eating in the right way. Often, we find on retreat, women actually aren't eating enough! I know that sounds strange but your body really needs regular meals in order to keep metabolism high. Start skipping meals on a regular basis and your body will think it's got a period of starvation coming up and will go into preservation mode, slowing metabolism and holding onto every last bit of fat.

 Copyright © 2016 Conscious Cooking

You've been told it time and time again, but breakfast really is the most important meal of the day. Breakfast not only sets you up physiologically for the day but it is also a great way to set your intention to have a day that puts your health and wellness at its heart.

Breakfast sets both your mood and your energy levels for the day. If you have a stingy, nutritionally vacant, meal (or no breakfast at all), you will feel deprived. When your blood sugar levels drop mid-morning (which they will), you will find you are craving a sugar, a caffeine hit or, quite likely, both together. It's no mystery why coffee and cakes/cookies/biscuits go hand in glove.

Our retreaters tell us that breakfast is often the most challenging meal. They can understand protein based meals for lunch and supper – but breakfast? It's a view that has been reinforced by many decades of reliance on boxed cereal as the basis for our breakfast.

Unfortunately cereal is probably one of the worse choices at breakfast. It is over-processed and over-sweetened. Don't for one moment let the "fortified with vitamins and minerals" fool you. Sugar is packed full of sugar and will cause spikes in blood glucose levels. To be very honest, the healthiest part of most breakfast cereals is the milk.

Protein, on the other hand, is the perfect way to start the day. A good, protein-packed breakfast, will keep your energy levels even and your mind focused.

When we say protein, we're not suggesting you scarf a fry up every morning – our recipe selection offers a wide variety of breakfast ideas – some quite unusual. Do keep an open mind - and open taste-buds!

Think you don't have time for breakfast? Think again. It takes only minutes to prepare a healthy, tasty, sustaining and nutrient-dense breakfast that will set you up for a successful day

 Copyright © 2016 Conscious Cooking

LUNCH

Lunch is the second most important meal of the day and, after breakfast, it should (ideally) be your second largest meal. Lunch is what stops you from free falling into a sugar craving mid-afternoon (much as we saw for breakfast). It is what gives you the energy to have a fully productive day.

Unfortunately lunch has become a bit of a dead zone. It's hard not to lay some blame at the doorstep of the "meal deal". It seems the meal deal has stitched up lunchtime with its standard offering of sandwich, crisps (or chocolate bar) and a fizzy drink. Of course, many meal deals do offer salad, fruit and water but, honestly, truly, do you go for that?

Frankly a takeaway sandwich is pretty much the worst lunch option you could find. Often it is a couple of slices of processed non-organic meat or dairy squashed between two slices of processed bread with the addition of a few salad items and a ton of mayo. Add crisps (dead calories) and a fizzy drink (packed with sugar or artificial sweeteners) and it's about as far from being a balanced meal as you could imagine.

Yes, you may need to plan ahead a little to have the ideal lunch but we promise it will be worthwhile. You can choose from our Light Bites or our Main Meals section. The latter includes plenty of dishes that can be made up in advance and frozen in batches. We're looking for a good mix of complex carbohydrate and protein, with lots of nutrient-packed vegetables. Lunch should be your most exciting meal of the day – the challenge is on!

SUPPER

By the time you have reached suppertime, your system is already preparing for bed. Once your main daily activities are finished, your brain starts wind down mode – this is perfect as it means that when you do go to bed, you are ready for sleep.

Unfortunately, most of us view supper as the main meal of the day. We eat our largest meals in the evening, and often quite late in the evening. This is not only bad news for your digestion but it's a total disaster if you're trying to lose weight. A large meal provides your body with a huge hit of energy (calories) and there is simply no way you are going to use it all up before you hit the hay. So what happens? The surplus will be stored as fat.

Now we're not saying you should never eat a big meal in the evening. Our culture, as it stands, makes a big deal out of eating out – it's seen as a treat and a way of socialising. Equally, supper is often the only time you can sit down with your partner or family – so supper is also about bonding.

A large blow-out once in a while is not going to be a problem (remember the 80:20 rule?). However if you're regularly eating your major meal at night, it's a recipe for disaster.

For the major part, your evening meal should be considered part of your wind-down routine. It's a time for light, soothing, nourishing food. You can still make it a sociable meal, just don't make it a heavy duty one. We'll show you plenty of ideas in the Light Bites recipe section. Of course, many people prefer to have their main meal at night, to fit in with family, or just from pure preference. Not a problem! Just be conscious and listen to your body.

 Copyright © 2016 Conscious Cooking

Healthy
SNACKS

Snacks are a vital part of your daily meal planner. But (and it's a big but) you need to snack wisely.

Most people who want to lose weight will steer clear of snacks. We've often been warned that snacking is the work of the devil. Wrong. Well-planned snacks (one mid-morning and one mid-afternoon) will stop your blood sugar levels diving. Why is this important? If your blood sugar starts dropping, your body will send you racing off to get a quick fix with a chocolate bar or a packet of biscuits.

Our recommendation is have a good breakfast, lunch and dinner and also to include a mid-afternoon snack. Don't go longer than three hours without eating (this is especially vital for women) or your blood sugar levels will drop too low and your body will give you a craving for something sweet to rectify the drop quickly.

Don't panic that you will gain weight by eating snacks. You won't – providing you eat the right sort of snacks. We want to educate you away from sweet, sugary snacks. Even fruit on its own will spike your blood sugar too much. You need to look for, as always, your best friend protein. In the recipe section we'll show you exactly how to snack smart.

If you know you have a slow metabolism – in other words, if you can virtually starve and still put on weight, then three meals a day plus one healthy snack is your best way forward. It sounds counter-intuitive but eating regularly, well-balanced nutritious meals and snacks, has been proven to boost metabolism. Add exercise and you're on the road to recovery. Trust us, we've put countless women on this journey, and the result are spectacular.

 Copyright © 2016 Conscious Cooking

Sweet
TREATS

On retreat we find that people usually most miss sweet treats when they're eating a healthy diet. We have become so used to equating something sweet with comfort or reward. Also many of us are conditioned to expect a burst of sweet on the palate after a meal.

In an ideal world you will educate your taste-buds away from sweet flavours but, hey, we're all human! When you are looking for something nutritious to satisfy your sweet tooth these quick and simple desserts are for you. All bar one of these is ready in 30 minutes or less and they are all packed full of healthy ingredients. The one that has a longer lead time actually only takes five minutes to prepare and then all you do is leave it to simmer...so nothing labour intensive here.

These are your go-to weeknight desserts that fit well within your new 80/20 lifestyle and I'm confident that you will enjoy then and find yourself coming back to them again and again. They taste great and can be served to anyone without apology. So, enjoy every mouthful...but do keep to the serving size. Even though they are made with healthy ingredient, if you let the portion sizes edge up you will soon find yourself feeling a little podgy.

 Copyright © 2016 Conscious Cooking

Conscious
PLANNING

You wouldn't run a marathon without training, would you? You wouldn't go into a big work project without preparation, would you? Yet when it comes to our food, we all too often just wing it.

We know from our years of success with our clients, that behind every success story is smart planning and preparation. We teach seven clear steps for success.

1. Set aside time once a week to plan your meals for the week ahead. This sounds like a hassle but it really is the best way to focus your intent. It also allows you to look at the week ahead and see what might possibly prove challenging. Are you travelling? Are you eating out, or going round to friends for supper? How much exercise are you doing? My planning ahead you can factor in all these plans.

2. Plan to have protein with every main meal. In total you should be aiming to have about 100g of protein per meal. Don't worry too much about this – the main point is that your daily nutrition is well balanced.

   I don't want to get too sciencey or turn you into calculator-toting freaks. When I say that you should aim to have about 100g of protein each meal this is the uncooked weight of your protein source. So, just as an example, you could have three eggs for brekkie, a can of tuna for lunch and a chicken breast for supper.

3. Think about what is seasonally available. You can get a quick guide on what is available at http://www.bbcgoodfood.com/seasonal-calendar/all Another good resource is www.eattheseasons.co.uk

   Having an organic vegetable box delivered is a great way to get a variety of seasonal vegetables – and may also challenge you to try new or different vegetables. Aim for at least five vegetable and no more than two fruits each day. This will help to keep your blood sugar levels in check while also ensuring that you get the full range of vitamins, minerals and other nutrients for a well-balanced body and mind.

 Copyright © 2016 Conscious Cooking

4. Factor in activity and exercise sessions too. If it's marked on your plan you are far more likely to actually do it! Plan to be as active every day – along with a good diet, it's the best thing you can do for your health. If you need to lose weight, it goes without saying that you will need to exercise as well as eat sensibly. The good news is that the latest research shows that you don't need to pound the treadmill for hours – short sharp busts of intense exercise are more effective – but you do need to sweat. Aim for 15-20 minutes exercise at least every other day as a good basis for health.

5. Invest in the right tools for your new healthy eating lifestyle. You will need Tupperware, travel cups/beakers/food storage bags and labels. Also check you have everything you need from the kitchen list in the Conscious Cooking section.

6. Write your plan down. It doesn't matter which medium you use – whatever works for you. A schedule on your PC and phone would be fine. Or print off a series of weekly food planners http://www.thebodyretreat.co.uk/the-body-retreat-meal-planners/ that you can fill in each week. We have found that our retreaters who had the best long term success all had their weekly meal plans on display in their kitchen as it helped them to stay focused.

7. Be realistic. It's tempting to go all out, to go to extremes but if you try to go too hard and fast you are more likely to run out of steam and lack the motivation to continue. Remember that you are not on a diet. Conscious Cooking is about making healthy conscious choices for life. Slow and steady wins the day here.

Conscious SHOPPING

At the Body Retreat we advocate mindfulness, consciousness, in everything. Just as you need to plan consciously, you also need to shop with mindfulness, awareness. Stop thinking of shopping as a chore; instead see it as an investment in your health. We've become so used to throwing food in a shopping trolley, or to clicking boxes mindlessly online, that we have lost our connection to the food we choose. Obviously you're busy, we're all busy, and we wouldn't advocate giving up the ease of online and supermarket shopping but use them carefully.

Let's look at conscious shopping.

1 Once a month do a big store cupboard/freezer/essentials shop. Online ordering is a godsend for this. Not only is it so much more convenient but it also means you can avoid the myriad tempting offers that lie in wait in store. Why is it that those offers are almost always on processed foods and sugary treats? We've never seen a 'Buy two lettuces, get a cucumber free' offer! That would be our kind of BOGOF offer! But that is an issue for another time; back to shopping. So, this is your chance to stock up on your essentials – see our shopping list in the appendix for a full list of our store cupboard essentials.

2 Several times a week, shop small, local and seasonally. You should have a plan for what you will be eating each week and you will have factored in your social, work and exercise requirements. You will also have checked out what is great to eat now as regards local seasonal produce, and your cupboards will be full of the essentials. So now you only need to top up with some seasonal goodies to finish off your meals. This makes sure that you are getting maximum freshness, maximum nutrition while also minimising waste.

3 Become label savvy. When you are next in the supermarket or even if ordering online, take a few moments to check out the labels of the foods you are choosing. You probably already know that ingredients are listed in order of volume in the product, so the biggest amount first. This is really important. You want the core produce to be the highest ingredient, so apple should be apples, not apple juice, not water and certainly not sugar. Next look for the sugar content (see point 4, next on the list). Count the number of ingredients in the product. If it's a list of spices and herbs, then fine but if it reads like a long chemical experiment, put it back on the shelf.

 Copyright © 2016 Conscious Cooking

4. Beware stealthy sugar. Sugar and sugar substitutes pop up in the most unusual places... so far we've found it in hummus, sausages, stock cubes and salad dressing. Often when manufacturers remove fat (which adds flavour and texture to a dish or product) they replace it with sugar. So for your next few shopping trips look at the labels and if you see sugar or one of its alternatives then put it back on the shelf.

5. Organic or not? This is a big question. In an ideal world we would not have to make this decision as all produce would be chemical free, but we live in the real world and have real and personal decision to make here, based on health, ethics and budget.

   At The Body Retreat we never compromise when it comes to meat and dairy. The antibiotics and hormones introduced into farming animals worry us. While the research community argues back and forth about acceptable levels in the human food chain, we are not happy to have any additional chemicals that may or may not impact our endocrine system in the produce we eat, or that we serve to our clients. We only eat and serve organic meat and dairy produce.

   Equally we don't compromise on organic tea and coffee. Tea and coffee are two of the most widely pesticide sprayed crops worldwide. In order to remove the pesticides you need to wash the produce. What happens when you wash tea and coffee? Well, you get tea and coffee. So the pesticides sprayed in the field end up in your cup.

   Now we come to fruit and vegetables. On retreat we tend to have organic produce where we possibly can. At home we encourage our retreaters to look at the annual review of the Clean 15 and the Dirty Dozen food lists. You can see more on www.ewg.org or www.eatingwell.com

   We recognise that organic food is more expensive and isn't always readily available but we encourage you to choose wisely.

6. Store cupboard essentials. Keep your cupboards stocked with a variety of produce so that you can quickly and conveniently rustle up a meal should you need to. Items like tins of pulses, tuna, tomatoes, anchovies, capers and olives alongside packs of whole grain rice, quinoa, and so on, mean that you always have the basics of a good meal to hand, even if you haven't been able to get to the shops. Again, see the shopping list at the back of the book.

7. Become choosy. No longer settle for food that does not inspire you, that you do not look forward to eating, that you know deep down does not nourish your body. So say no to yellow labels, BOGOF offers and meal deals. Choose to be choosy.

Conscious COOKING

Do you find cooking a chore? It's time to develop a whole new mind-set. In the past, cooking was taken slowly, it almost become a meditation. Many traditional cultures still cook this way – pouring love, comfort, caring and attention to the foods they prepare. This is real 'soul food' – nourishing not just body, but mind, emotion and soul. Let's look at how to cook modern soul food, when you're short on time.

1. **ENJOY YOURSELF.** Yes, at first when you are mastering a new recipe or a new way of eating, it can feel clunky and even a little uncomfortable. But like any habit it does not take very long before you find yourself cooking instinctively. So keep it simple but consistent in the kitchen and your confidence levels will soon go through the roof.

2. **SAVE TIME WITH PREP.** Very often it is the preparation of ingredients that takes the time, not the actual cooking or assembly of a dish. So give yourself a head start. Once you have completed your weekly meal planner (see Conscious Planning) you will get a sense of how many of each ingredient you need. So why not spend 30 minutes on a Sunday night and chop up a few onions, peppers, carrots etc. and then individually bag them up and put them in the fridge so that when you are ready to cook the bulk of your prep is done. Note: you will need to do this every 3-4 days as the chopped ingredients will not hold the freshness as well as the whole foods.

3. **COOK CLEAN.** The cleanest ways to cook are steaming, blanching, grilling and baking. All these methods help to keep nutrients in the foods you have chosen. So it's goodbye to frying, in particular deep frying. Don't panic – as you'll find when you start following our recipes, you won't miss the big fry.

4. **NO MICROWAVING.** Except in emergencies get out of the microwave habit. It is a time saver for sure but recent research suggests that microwaved food has lost up to 95 percent of its nutrients.

5. GET TOOLED UP.
There are a few bits of kit that every cook needs in their kitchen.

- 1 great cook's knife
- 1 decent/heavy chopping board
- 1 small omelette size pan
- 1 decent potato peeler (not so much for the spud but rather for shaving cheese and making vegetable noodles)
- Measuring spoons
- Digital scales
- A high powered blender. Makes blitzing nuts, seeds and vegetables easy.

6. THINK ABOUT THE MINDFUL MOUTHFUL.
When we eat we want to be sensually engaged with what is going on in our mouths. To help that process take a little time to create dishes that contain different textures, tastes, temperatures and even sounds. You will notice in some of the recipes that ingredients are often added in random order – this is to preserve the nutritional value of the foods and also to provide a depth of experience to the palate. Think this sounds airy fairy? Consider stew – if you just bung all the ingredients in together, you end up with a humungous mush. It may be a very tasty mush but that is not what Conscious Cooking is about. Instead we vary when we add certain ingredients so that the stew has mushy bits and crunchy bits, soft juicy bits and crisper crunchier bits – all adding up to a more interesting and nutritious mouthful.

7. MAXIMISE YOUR TIME IN THE KITCHEN.
I love to cook, it makes me happy, it relaxes me and I enjoy the pleasure of sitting to eat what I have prepared. I know that not everyone shares my view. For some, cooking and time in the kitchen is a necessary evil. So maximise your output when in the kitchen.

- Making a roast? Pop a couple of whole bell peppers into the oven. No oil, no seasoning, just leave them for about 20 minutes to soften. Then when cool pop into a bag and into the fridge. Now you have roasted peppers you can use in salads, soups or dips through the week.

- Repeat with roast vegetables. Don't you hate it when you buy beetroots or carrots etc. and when you fish them out of the fridge to cook they have gone a bit soft? Hate that! So instead pop a few carrots, parsnips, beetroots, even potatoes on a baking sheet and cook for about 15 minutes. When cool, put in bags in the fridge or you can even pop in to the freezer.

Conscious EATING

At The Body Retreat we encourage all our retreaters to eat consciously. All too often we eat when we are fully engaged in another activity and the practice of eating becomes robotic; sometimes we just shovel food from plate to mouth. In contrast we're looking to enjoy our food, to feel nourished by food. So we need to start a practice of conscious eating, of sitting down for each and every meal and every snack. This way we develop a good relationship with food and we learn how to feel in control around food.

This list of instructions may seem a little strange at first: we are so used to wolfing down our food, barely realising what we are eating. However, if you practice these steps conscientiously, you will soon find that they become second nature.

1. **POSTURE RESET.** Sit down and feel your feet set firmly on the floor. Sit up straight (this helps digestion) – imagine there's a string fastened to the very top of your head gently tugging your body erect. Take three deep slow breaths.

   On every out breath roll your shoulder blades down and back. Yawn widely to release any tension in your jaw.

2. **CHECK YOUR HUNGER SCALE.** Listen to your body. On a scale of one to ten, how hungry does your body feel? Really listen.

3. **LOOK AT YOUR PLATE.** Be mindful of the food on your plate, appreciating the colours and textures. Really notice what you're going to be eating.

4. **SMELL YOUR FOOD.** You can either sniff the plate or your first fork/spoonful. This engages your olfactory senses and wakes up your digestive system. Your nose will be able to detect the kind of food on your fork and will send messages for the correct enzymes to be released to deal with the type of food you're eating.

    Copyright © 2016 Conscious Cooking

5. **CHEW SLOWLY AND MINDFULLY.** Really savour the taste, temperature and textures of the food you're eating. Chew your food until it is virtually liquid. Remember that digestion begins in the mouth. Don't even think of eating any more until your mouth is completely clear.

6. **PLACE YOUR CUTLERY DOWN BETWEEN EACH AND EVERY MOUTHFUL.** This stops you mindlessly gulping down your food. It also gives you a chance, between each mouthful, to consider if you're starting to feel full.

7. **STOP EATING WHEN YOU FEEL SATISFIED, NOT FULL.** This can be hard at first. We are so unused to listening to our bodies and to eating according to real hunger. Most of us were brought up to eat everything on our plate. But just start being aware of how you're feeling.

8. **ALWAYS LEAVE SOMETHING ON YOUR PLATE.** It doesn't have to be a lot and, yes, it's fine to leave something you don't particularly like. This is a psychological pointer, signalling to your subconscious that you don't have to eat everything put in front of you. You control your plate; your plate does not control you!

9. **DON'T DRINK WATER WITH YOUR MEAL.** This may come as a surprise, as we've been told to drink water to 'fill us up' and water is served as a matter of course at most restaurants and dining table. Too much water will dilute the digestive enzymes which are so important to absorption of energy and nutrients form the food you have eaten.

RECIPES

- **Perfection is almost never needed.** The recipes do not have to be followed precisely. We are not baking a cake, this is not chemistry, so relax into the recipe and you will find your intuition kicks in. If you need to adapt or fudge a recipe in some way you will feel confident to do it in a way that maintains the healthy principles of Conscious Cooking.

- **Make sensible swaps.** When it does come to making substitutions in recipes for any reason, make your choice of alternative wisely. For example if a recipe calls for spinach then swap it for another leafy green vegetable, not peas which are higher in sugar.

- **Most recipes are low in gluten and grains and sugars.**

- **More is more.** You will find that I use a number of core ingredients in my staple recipes, this means that you do not buy a jar or bag of produce that you only need for one recipe. Rather you will use them more often so there is less wastage all round.

- **Eat the whole food.** Providing you're using organic produce, use the skin, fat, rind of the majority of products. A lot of nutrients are held in the skin of fruits and vegetables for example. And, yes, a bit of crispy bacon fat from time to time is absolutely fine – it satisfies your psychological need for a treat, while (on a nutritional level) the fat helps you to feel fuller and more satisfied for longer.

- **Banish all low fat and sugar-free foods.** Fake foods really aren't kind to your body. Fat has been demonised for years, quite unfairly. Of course it depends on the kind of fat you're eating but natural fat in food is not your enemy. In low fat or sugar free foods manufacturers need to replace the fats and sugars with artificial sweeteners and additives to give texture and taste. Once again, you're looking at a pile of chemical nasties. Your body simply doesn't know how to handle these fake foods. Much better to have a little of the real deal than a lot of the fake stuff.

 Copyright © 2016 Conscious Cooking

 Copyright © 2016 Conscious Cooking

Top TIPS

- A handful of walnuts gives nearly 90 percent of your daily omega 3 requirement.

- Flaxseed does more than just add a fibre boost to your meal or smoothie. As well as slowing down the absorption of natural sugars, it also gives a dose of essential fatty acids.

- Soak seeds and nuts overnight if you can - this makes them more digestible and increases nutritional content.

- Raspberries contain the most fibre of any berry, coming in at 8gms of fibre per cup.

- Lentils provide iron and foliate and are a great source of protein.

- Leeks, garlic and onions help to protect against inflammation. However some people who are fructose intolerant find they increase wind.

- Despite the name, buckwheat is actually a seed and can help lower blood pressure and cholesterol.

- Did you know that broccoli has more vitamin C than an orange?

- Berries have less fructose and more anti-oxidants than fruits like mango or banana and so can be enjoyed regularly.

- Most the nutrients of potato are found just under the skin, so scrub rather than peel where possible

- Don't throw out brown bananas, peel and chop and pop in a freezer bag. Just one cube of frozen ripe banana makes a great sweet addition to a smoothie and gives a great creamy texture.

 Copyright © 2016 Conscious Cooking

THE RECIPES

BREAKFAST

Porridge
Buckwheat Breakfast
Green Goodness Smoothie
On the Go Smoothie
Breakfast Zinger Juice
Bircher Muesli
Baked Granola
Warm Citrus Compote
On the Go Fritters
Pumpkin Pancakes
Spinach & Feta Scramble
Baked Egg & Peppers
Superfruit & Seed Salad
Avocado on Toast

LIGHT BITES

Soups, Salads & Sides
Thai Beef Salad
Pear & Roquefort Salad
Wholefood Salad
Scallop & Chorizo Salad
Spanish Salad
Prawn, Avocado & Grapefruit Salad
Warm Coronation Salad
Broccoli, Almond & Stilton Soup
Thai Butternut Squash Soup
Roast Yellow Pepper Soup
Tomato & Chickpea Soup
Parsnip & Apple Soup
Cream of Chicken & Sweetcorn Soup
Courgette & Pea Frittata
Mushroom Ragout
Veggie Parcels

39   Copyright © 2016 Conscious Cooking

MAIN DISHES

Beef Stifado
Medieval Spiced Pork
Duck Breast with Lime & Honey
Moroccan Spiced Chicken
Lamb with Herbs & Lemons
Lamb Koftas
Toulouse Sausage Cassoulet
Caponata
Lemon Chicken Stir-fry
Turkey Meatballs & Courgetini
Sea Bass & Fennel
Fish Pie
Pepper Crusted Fish
Mushroom Barley Risotto
Spiced Yellow Pea Curry
Moroccan Bean Stew

SNACKS

Power Balls
Trail Mix
Hummus
Oat Bars
Flapjack
Apple & Celery Sandwich
Power Juice
Citrus Green Tea Refresher

SWEET TREATS

Mango & Ginger Pudding
Citrus Yoghurt Fool
Fruit Crumble
Rhubarb & Orange Posset
Chocolate Mouse
Coconut Rice Pudding

 Copyright © 2016 Conscious Cooking

The
RECIPES

ENERGIZING BREAKFASTS

What you eat for breakfast literally can determine how your whole day pans out. It's your chance to make each and every day a great one.

Aim to eat within about an hour of waking, if you are looking to shed unwanted weight then exercise first thing before you break your fast. On retreat we always have an exercise class before breakfast – not a long or heavy duty one but it gets everyone moving and starts the day on a high. Plus, of course, everyone really enjoys breakfast afterwards!

Some people say they don't have time for breakfast – in which case, we say 'look at our recipes' as there are lots that honestly take next to no time.

However some women on our retreats say that they just can't face breakfast, that they can't stomach food first thing in the morning. If that's you, then start your day with hot water and the juice of half a lemon. This will rehydrate you, support your liver and wake your taste buds. Then take an apple and a small handful of nuts with you to eat when you are ready. Make sure that you make time to eat a proper breakfast later in the morning. Don't simply snack or you will find yourself in a blood sugar nose dive by lunchtime.

Okay, time to wake up and discover some of the fastest, tastiest ways to kickstart your morning!

The problem with porridge is that often it is served with fruit and honey (or sugar and milk) which takes the slow release from oats and speeds up the energy release. To make sure you are sustained all morning, add seeds and nuts as they act to slow down the absorption of the natural sugars.

 Copyright © 2016 Conscious Cooking

Porridge with apple and
CINNAMON

THIS IS SO SIMPLE YET IT IS ALWAYS A WINNER.

Makes one serving.

40 g (1.5 oz) (1/2 cup) whole jumbo porridge oats

150 ml (5 fl oz) water

100 ml (3.5 fl oz) unsweetened almond milk

½ teaspoon cinnamon

1 teaspoon ground flax seed

2 drops vanilla extract

120 g (4 oz) (1 ¼ cup) chopped almonds

15 ml (0.5 fl oz) organic apple, grated (leave the skin on)

1. Place all ingredients except the apple into a pan on the stove and gently bring to a light boil. Stir until the mixture thickens (about five minutes), then add the apple and stir through.

2. Serve with grated apple and chopped almonds on top.

3. Note: Always use organic apples. The chemicals sprayed on non-organic apples doesn't just stay in the skin but penetrates right through the apple.

Breakfast Smoothies & JUICES

We often have clients on retreat who tell us that they never have time for breakfast.

Mornings can be really busy for sure, but this breakfast takes less than a minute to prepare

 Copyright © 2016 Conscious Cooking

Green Goodness Smoothie

This is green powerhouse of a smoothie, packed with nutrients and plant protein. The peanut butter gives it an unctuous, satisfying texture.

Makes one serving.

Handful fresh baby spinach

½ cup almond milk (125 ml) (4 fl oz)

1 tbsp peanut butter

1 teaspoon chia seeds

1 teaspoon ground flaxseed

Drop vanilla extract

Put all ingredients in a blender and blend until smooth.

On the Go Breakfast Smoothie

This smoothie really is a meal in a flask. It's thick, tasty and deeply satisfying and sustaining. Our go-to recipe when we have a busy schedule.

Makes one serving.

1 heaped tbsp rolled porridge oats

1 teaspoon ground flaxseed

½ medium banana

½ cup unsweetened almond milk (125 ml) (4 fl oz) (or make your own)

1 tbsp natural yoghurt

1 tbsp coconut water

Put all ingredients in a blender and blend until smooth.

 Copyright © 2016 Conscious Cooking

Breakfast Szinger
JUICE

One of my favourite juices. This is sharp, clean and sweet. It is also the most amazing colour which cannot help but make you smile. Just watch out for the orange moustache!

Makes two servings

4 large organic carrots

1 large orange

1 large lemon

¼ inch fresh ginger

½ tsp Psyllium husks

Simply wash your carrots, no need to peel or chop off the ends, and then just pop them straight in the machine. Juice all ingredients together and serve immediately with a small handful of cashew nuts to help balance the naturally high sugar of this juice.

 Copyright © 2016 Conscious Cooking

Many people think buckwheat is a grain but it is actually a fruit seed, which makes it a perfect choice if you are looking to reduce your grain consumption. It has a distinctive nutty almond sweet taste. Try it, you might surprise yourself.

Buckwheat
BREAKFAST

Makes one serving

1 tbsp raw buckwheat groats

Handful of summer fruits (raspberries, blueberries, strawberries, black or red-currants etc.)

½ banana, roughly chopped

1 tbsp seed mixture (3 parts linseed: 1 part sesame: 1 part pumpkin: 1 part sunflower)

Handful of raisins

1. Put the buckwheat in a small saucepan and cover with about ½ cm (0.2") of water. Gently boil off the water until it has evaporated but the buckwheat has not stuck to the saucepan.

2. Grind up the seed mixture finely. Add the raisins and grind again.

3. Put all the ingredients into a serving bowl and lightly combine.

4. You might want to add a splash of hot milk to loosen off the mix.

 Copyright © 2016 Conscious Cooking

This is another amazing time-saving breakfast. It's an old classic that is now regaining in popularity – with great reason. This will keep in a sealed container in the fridge for 2-3 days. This breakfast is only sweetened by the apple juice, nuts and vanilla extract

 Copyright © 2016 Conscious Cooking

Bircher MUESLI

Makes around six servings

200 g (7 oz) (2 cups) rolled oats

50 g (1.5 oz) (1/3 cup) mixed seeds

200 ml (7 fl oz) cold milk (skimmed, soy or rice)

80 ml (2.8 fl oz) apple juice

150 g (5 oz) natural yogurt

1 large organic Granny Smith apple, cored and roughly grated

100 g (3.5 oz) (1 cup) mixed berries (mashed)

25 g (1 oz) (1.5 tbsp) honey

Handful raisins

½ teaspoon vanilla extract

60 g (2.5 oz) (1/2 cup) walnuts, lightly toasted and roughly chopped

1. Put the oats and seeds in a large mixing bowl and add the milk and apple juice.

2. Stir and leave aside for at least ten minutes to soften or leave them to soak overnight in the fridge, which will soften them up a bit more.

3. When ready to serve, add the yoghurt, grated apple, mashed berries, honey, raisins and vanilla.

4. Stir and transfer to serving bowls.

5. Top with walnuts.

 Copyright © 2016 Conscious Cooking

I often get creative with my granola but this is my basic recipe. Once you have mastered this then you can switch nuts, fruits, flavourings etc.

The problem with many shop-bought granolas is that they are very high in sugars and, as we have already seen, even natural sugars will impact your energy levels and hormones.

This granola is based on healthy grains, seeds and nuts which offer a slow release of energy to keep you balanced all morning.

You will never miss the added sweetness.

 Copyright © 2016 Conscious Cooking

Baked GRANOLA

Makes 10 -12 servings

(will keep in an air tight jar for up to two weeks)

Preheat the oven to 160°C/320°F/gas mark 3

100 g (3.5 oz) (1 cup) rye flakes

100 g (3.5 oz) (1 cup) jumbo oats

50 g (2 oz) (1/2 cup) whole unblanched almonds

50 ml (1.5 fl oz) rapeseed oil

20 ml (0.6 fl oz) pure maple syrup
(or honey and cinnamon)*

100 g (3.5 oz) (1 cup) buckwheat grouts

50 g (2 oz) (1/3 cup) mixed seeds

50 g (2 oz) (1/3 cup) chopped apricots

25 g (1 oz) (1/4 cup) dried cranberries

50 g (2 oz) (2/3 cup) unsweetened dry sliced coconut (not desiccated)

Pinch coarse sea salt

* You can replace the maple syrup with a tablespoon of honey and a generous sprinkle of cinnamon.

1. Place the rye flakes, oats and almonds in a bowl and mix.
2. Meanwhile mix together the rapeseed oil and syrup.
3. Pour over the flake and nut mix.
4. Mix thoroughly with your hands.
5. Spread the flake and nut mix evenly on a lined baking tray and sprinkle with a pinch of sea salt.
6. Cook in the oven for about 20 minutes, stirring occasionally until the whole mix is a nice golden colour.
7. Add the remaining ingredients and cook for a further five minutes.
8. Serve with natural yogurt or your milk of choice.

   Copyright © 2016 Conscious Cooking

This is one of my all-time favourite breakfasts. I lost the recipe and tried for many years to recreate it then by a stroke of luck I found the recipe again to realise that what was missing was the tinned pineapple. You can use fresh pineapple but the tinned stuff really adds a certain something.

52   Copyright © 2016 Conscious Cooking

Warm Citrus Breakfast
COMPOTE

Makes two servings

3 dried apricots

1 teaspoon mixed seeds

½ orange

½ red grapefruit

3 dates

20 g (3/4 oz) (1/10 cup) sultanas

1 ring pineapple (tinned or fresh*)

1 teaspoon mixed spice

20 g (3/4 oz) (1/4 cup) flaked or chopped almonds

* If you are using fresh pineapple you will also need a glug of orange juice
Natural yogurt to serve.

1. Place the dried fruit and seeds in a splash of the pineapple or orange juice and leave to soak for half an hour or more (you can do this overnight if you wish).

2. Peel and chop the fresh fruit into small bite size chunks.

3. Add the fresh fruit to the dried fruit and the mixed spice in a small pan and gentle heat on the stove for about ten minutes.

4. You will notice that at this stage the dried fruits start to break down and produce a lovely caramel colour and thicken the sauce slightly, but the fruit still retains its shape. We're not looking for mush here so do not boil!

5. Next add the almonds and stir.

6. Leave to simmer while you get the yogurt ready.

7. Serve while still warm on top of two tablespoons (about 80 ml) of natural yogurt.

   Copyright © 2016 Conscious Cooking

Too busy for breakfast? Make these up the night before and then you have a tasty on-the-go breakfast the next day. You can also make up these little portable fritters for picnics or to take with you when travelling...beats an aeroplane sandwich hands down.

 Copyright © 2016 Conscious Cooking

On The Go Breakfast
FRITTERS

Makes two servings

Preheat oven to 170°C/325°F/gas mark 3

1 tbsp rapeseed oil

2 scallions, finely chopped

3 broccoli florets, finely chopped

20 g (3/4 oz) (2 tbsp) peas

2 medium eggs

Handful fresh dill

40 g (1½ oz) feta cheese

Salt and black pepper

1. Grease the muffin tray with a little of the oil and set aside.

2. Heat the remaining oil in a pan and gently soften the scallions for one to two minutes.

3. Add the broccoli and peas and warm through.

4. Beat the eggs in a jug and add the soft vegetables, crumble in the feta and add the chopped dill.

5. Season with salt and black pepper.

6. Pour into the greased muffin tray.

7. Bake in the oven for about 30 minutes until set and slightly springy to the touch.

8. Pop in a Tupperware box or cover with tin foil and they're ready to go.

 Copyright © 2016 Conscious Cooking

Pumpkin
PANCAKE

These make the perfect weekend breakfast. Once you try these filling pancakes you will never look at pancakes in the same way again.

Pumpkin is incredibly rich in antioxidants and vitamins and gives a real boost to your weekend breakfast.

Makes two servings

Pre heat oven to

180ºC/350ºF/gas mark 4

150g (5oz) (1 cup) of mashed baked pumpkin (see below)

150g (5oz) (1 cup) of gluten free flour – spelt or rye etc.

1 teaspoon gluten free baking powder

1 teaspoon allspice

½ teaspoon ground cinnamon

(you can vary the spices for individual taste)

½ teaspoon ground ginger

Pinch of salt

1 egg, separated

250ml (8 fl oz) (1 cup) of milk – organic soya or almond milk

2 tbsp rapeseed oil

    Copyright © 2016 Conscious Cooking

1. Peel and slice approximately 150 g (5 oz) of pumpkin and place on a dry baking tray lined with baking parchment.

2. Bake in the oven for about 20 minutes until soft but not browned.

3. (Do not boil the pumpkin as it will take on a more watery consistency and will not be fluffy).

4. Meanwhile in a large bowl mix the dry ingredients – the flour, baking powder, spices and salt.

5. Separate the egg and add the yolk to the milk – keep the white separate to whisk later.

6. When the pumpkin is cooked, mash to a purée and then add to the dry ingredients.

7. Pour the milk and egg mixture onto the dry pumpkin mix to make a thick batter. You may not need all the milk mix so pour in glug by glug.

8. Whisk up the egg white and then fold into your batter mix with a metal spoon to keep the air in. This makes for lighter, fluffier pancakes.

9. Heat a tablespoon of rapeseed oil in a large frying pan.

10. When hot, dollop in the batter mix and cook four pancakes at a time.

11. Use a pallet knife or fish slice to turn after about a minute to cook the other side.

12. Place the first four pancakes to one side or in a warm oven while you repeat for the next pancakes.

13. A serving is one large or two small pancakes served with two rashers of grilled streaky bacon, one sliced strawberry and a teaspoon of maple syrup – just a teaspoon now!

 Copyright © 2016 Conscious Cooking

We have become a nation of cereal munchers thanks to how the advertisers like to portray breakfast. As I've already explained, cereal is probably the last thing you want to be eating. If you want to leave the table satisfied and be able to pass on the biscuit tin at elevens then make eggs a staple part of your breakfast.

Copyright © 2016 Conscious Cooking

Spinach SCRAMBLE

Makes one serving

1 teaspoon rapeseed oil
2 handfuls baby leaf spinach
2 free range eggs
50 g (1.5 oz) (1/3 cup) feta, cubed
Salt & pepper
Small bunch fresh chives, snipped
Slice of rye toast to serve

1. Heat the oil in a pan over a medium heat.

2. Add the spinach and cook for a minute or two until wilted.

3. In a bowl crack the eggs and season with salt and pepper, whisk them together.

4. Add the eggs to the pan and add the feta cubes.

5. Gently stir over a medium low heat until the eggs are cooked.

6. Sprinkle with the snipped chives on half a slice of rye toast.

 Copyright © 2016 Conscious Cooking

This is based on a North African dish called shakshuka, but variations on it can be found all around the Med and over into North Africa.

We have this for breakfast on the first morning of every Andalusian Retreat. It is such a bright and sunny dish, with real depth of flavour – Spain on a plate.

Yes, it takes 1½ hours to make, but don't let that put you off. It's really only chopping and then you just let it gently cook away. Just before you are about to serve, it will take about 8–10 minutes of attention while it bakes.

60   Copyright © 2016 Conscious Cooking

Baked Egg and PEPPERS

Makes four servings

Preheat the oven to
200°C/400°F/fan180°C/gas mark 6

4 garlic cloves

1 hot red chilli (optional)

2 tbsp olive oil

2 red onions, roughly sliced

2 red peppers, roughly sliced

1 yellow pepper, roughly sliced

1 green pepper, roughly sliced

1/2 teaspoon salt

400g (14 oz) can (2 cups) plum tomatoes

2 tbsp balsamic vinegar

Pepper

Small handful baby spinach

4 eggs

Fresh parsley, coriander or dill to garnish

1. Chop the garlic and chilli (if using), until you have a rough paste.

2. Heat the oil in a large, deep frying pan, add the garlic and chilli and fry very briefly.

3. Add the onions, peppers and salt.

4. Stir once, cover, lower the heat and sweat for 10-15 minutes, or until it just starts to catch a little.

5. Meanwhile, drain the tomatoes and squish them to remove excess juice.

6. Add the pulp and vinegar to the pan, reduce the heat to low and cook for about 45 minutes, stirring occasionally. The peppers must be soft enough to break with a spoon, and the juices should be reduced, dark and glossy.

7. Season to taste.

8. Mix the spinach through the pepper mix.

9. Divide the vegetables between dishes, make a dip in each and break in an egg.

10. Bake for 8-10 minutes, until the egg is just setting. Leave the yolk soft as it will enrich the peppers when it breaks.

11. Garnish with herbs.

 Copyright © 2016 Conscious Cooking

This is probably one of my all-time favourite things to eat. It is so simple it seems churlish to call it a recipe but I've included it as I really would love people to eat more avocados. After many years of "fat phobia" the poor old avocado has had such a bad rap, but it's a true superfood.

 Copyright © 2016 Conscious Cooking

Avocado
TOAST

Makes one serving

1 slice rye bread

½ ripe avocado

Juice of fresh lemon

Dried chilli flakes

Fresh dill

10g/2 tsp mixed seeds

Black pepper

1. To construct this delicacy you simply pop the bread into the toaster while you scoop out the avocado flesh and mash up in a cup with a generous squeeze of lemon juice and little sprinkle of dried chilli flakes and black pepper (to your own personal taste).

2. When the toast is done just pile up the avocado on top of the bread, sprinkle with the seeds and more chilli flakes.

3. If you want to make this meal a feast add a soft poached egg on top.

Light Fruit and
SEEDS SALAD

This is a light and delicious fruit salad – a rainbow of colours on the plate and packed with antioxidants. It's a great way to kickstart your day as it makes an uplifting breakfast. However, if it were purely fruit you would be in danger of a mid-morning sugar slump so that's where the nuts and seeds come in. The additional fibre, fat and protein are necessary to create that balance: miss them off and you'll be reaching for a muffin mid morning

Makes four servings

1 organic apple, skin on and cubed

½ pomegranate – just the seeds

¼ watermelon, cubed

1 slice fresh pineapple, cubed

50g blueberries

¼ mango, cubed

40g walnuts

20g sunflower and pumpkin seeds

Juice and zest of a fresh lime

1. Cut all fruits and arrange on plates, sprinkle with seeds and a little freshly squeezed lime juice and zest and serve. We often serve this on retreat with a dollop of natural yoghurt on the side. We serve on a plate rather than in breakfast bowls to ensure we don't just end up shovelling big spoonfuls of fruit. Instead we need to observe and choose each fruit in a mindful way.

 Copyright © 2016 Conscious Cooking

Light BITES

Quick to prepare, easy to transport and light on the digestive system these meals are perfect at any time of the day. They make a great lunch option or a light meal at the end of a long and busy day.

A word about salads... I grew up in a household where salad was boring – basically a dull mix of iceberg lettuce, tomato and cucumber. Hardly the stuff of inspiration. But it made me think – there has to be better, more interesting ways to work with leaves! Hence began my experimentation with all things salad.

These six salads are all well-balanced and contain all the macronutrients you need all on one plate.

The secret to a great salad is to buy the best quality raw ingredients you can afford.

An organic home grown tomato will always outdo a cheap imported tasteless water filled orb. That can be tough to find, of course, unless you have your own greenhouse but, generally speaking, tomatoes 'on the vine' have much more taste than their separated at birth counterparts.

When it comes to dressings, you really don't need to be too fancy. There is little to beat a good quality oil, lemon and a little salt and pepper.

Eating red meat at night can be very taxing on the digestive system. Did you know it can take up to four days to fully digest beef steak? It takes about 6 – 8 hours to pass through the stomach into the intestines. Sorry, I know you don't really want this image as you contemplate your lunch! But it's good to know that it's not just what you eat but how and when you eat that helps your digestions. Eating red meat at night means that as you go to bed it will still be doing its digestive thing. I would recommend that you eat red meat earlier in the day and so give your body the opportunity to catch up. You will sleep much better

By the way, this is a great way to use up leftover roast beef

 Copyright © 2016 Conscious Cooking

Thai Beef
SALAD

Makes four servings

1 tbsp Thai fragrant rice

450 g (1 lb) (2 cups) beef (can use fillet, beef steak or left over roast beef)

4 shallots or ½ onion

4 spring onions

8 tbsp beef stock

4 tbsp fish sauce

Juice of 1 lemon or lime

1 teaspoon crushed dried chillies or chilli powder

2 teaspoons caster sugar

4 tbsp coriander, chopped

Green salad: 4 large handfuls watercress

1 green pepper, thinly sliced

50 g (1.5 oz) (1/3 cup) peas, frozen

1. Cook rice in a dry frying pan for five minutes until golden brown. Keep stirring so it doesn't burn.

2. Grind rice in a pestle and mortar.

3. Pre-heat the grill to high and grill the meat for two to three minutes each side, close to the heat.

4. Slice thinly and leave to one side.

5. Chop shallots and slice spring onions. Put to one side.

6. Put the stock, fish sauce, juice, chilli and sugar in a wok and bring to the boil.

7. Add the beef, shallots, rice, onions and coriander.

8. Stir and heat for a few seconds only.

9. Serve immediately on the green salad.

 Copyright © 2016 Conscious Cooking

Pear and Roquefort
SALAD

This is a fabulous mix – the sweetness of the pear is offset by the salty, tart Roquefort and the crunch of walnuts.

Makes four servings

2 pears, cored and thinly sliced

2 tbsp rapeseed oil

1 tbsp white wine vinegar

1 teaspoon honey

Salt and pepper

1 bag mixed salad leaves

100 g (3.5 oz) (1 cup) Roquefort cheese

40 g (1½ oz) (1/3 cup) walnut halves

1. Put a griddle pan on to heat.

2. Place the pear slices into a bowl and drizzle with 1 teaspoon of the rapeseed oil.

3. Cook the pear slices in batches for one minute each side until golden griddle lines are formed, then leave to rest on the side under foil.

4. Mix the remaining oil, vinegar, honey, salt and pepper together.

5. Layer the leaves and pear slices on the plates.

6. Crumble the Roquefort cheese over.

7. In a dry pan warm the walnut halves then sprinkle them on top of the salad.

8. Drizzle each plate with a little dressing.

   Copyright © 2016 Conscious Cooking

Whole food
SALAD

If you generally find salads too meagre and unsatisfying, this is the dish that will change your mind. The mix of beans, quinoa (packed with protein) and feta is truly sustaining.

Makes two servings

80 g (3 oz) (1/2 cup) soy beans, defrosted

80 g (3 oz) (1/2 cup) quinoa, cooked al dente, (about 10 minutes)

50 g (2 oz) ¼ cup) cannellini beans, drained

4 broccoli florets, cooked al dente

50 g (2 oz) (1/2 cup) feta cheese

½ pomegranate, seeded

20 g (3/4 oz) (1 ½ tbsp) golden raisins

¼ cucumber, chopped

1. 2 tbsp yogurt

2. 2 tbsp rapeseed oil

3. Juice of ½ a lemon

4. Salt and black pepper

5. Lettuce to serve.

6. Allow all the cooked ingredients to cool, then combine all the main ingredients.

7. Serve on a bed of lettuce and drizzle over the dressing.

    Copyright © 2016 Conscious Cooking

Scallop and
CHORIZO SALAD

Makes four servings

12 scallops

Good pinch smoked paprika

1 tbsp olive oil, plus extra for drizzling

100 g (3.5 oz) (½ cup) chorizo, sliced into rings

½ red onion, finely chopped

½ lime, cut into wedges

Bag of salad leaves – watercress or rocket work well with their peppery taste.

1. Start by whisking together the dressing ingredients, season with salt and pepper.

2. Score a criss-cross on the bottoms of your scallops with a sharp knife, and rub all over with paprika.

3. Heat the oil in a frying pan over a medium heat.

4. Add the chorizo and fry until it starts to crisp and release its juices.

5. Now add the onion to the pan with the chorizo and continue to fry for three or four more minutes to soften.

6. Remove the chorizo and onion and leave to one side.

7. Add the scallops to the chorizo oils and juices in the pan and gently fry on each side for two to three minutes.

8. Remove and squeeze over the lime.

9. Serve on a bed of salad leaves, drizzled with the juices from the pan.

 Copyright © 2016 Conscious Cooking

Another salad with a decidedly Spanish twist. We love our summer retreats in Andalusia and it's an endless source of inspiration to me. This salad is gutsy and robust. If you would like to make a vegetarian version, just lose the anchovies (a little smoked tofu could work well, if you wanted to up the protein content). If you would like to make a vegetarian version, just lose the anchovies (a little smoked tofu could work well, if you wanted to up the protein content

 Copyright © 2016 Conscious Cooking

Ensalada ESPAÑOL

Makes four servings

Preheat the oven to 200°C/400°F/gas mark 6

1 large red pepper, roasted & chopped

1 large green pepper, roasted & chopped

8 anchovy fillets

Head of Romaine lettuce, roughly chopped

3 spring onions, chopped

½ cucumber, chopped

1 x 400 g (14 oz) (2 cups) tin chick peas, drained

Large handful chopped parsley

Dressing:

1 tbsp oil from the anchovy fillets

1 tbsp raw honey

1 tbsp sherry vinegar

2 tbsp cold pressed rapeseed oil

½ tsp sweet paprika

1. Cut each pepper in half, smear with a little of the anchovy oil, place on a baking tray and bake in a hot oven for 15-20 minutes.

2. Meanwhile, make up the dressing and set to one side to allow the flavours to develop.

3. Combine the salad veggies except for the chickpeas.

4. When the peppers are soft and a little charred, cut into slices.

5. Add the dressing to the chickpeas and coat generously.

6. Plate up the salad veggies, top with the roast pepper slices and finally sprinkle over the chickpeas and parsley.

 Copyright © 2016 Conscious Cooking

This is an elegant salad, absolutely perfect for summer days or picnics. The sweet-sharp grapefruit cuts through the unctuousness of the avocado and prawns and the chilli gives it a subtle kick! Don't be scared of avocados – yes, they are high in fat but it's the kind of fat that is really healthy and which also keeps you satisfied for longer.

74   Copyright © 2016 Conscious Cooking

Prawn avocado and Grapefruit Salad with Sweet
CHILLI DRESSING

Makes two servings

1 ruby or pink grapefruit

1 avocado

250 g (9 oz) (1 cup) king prawns

1 tbsp grapeseed oil

½ garlic clove, crushed

½ teaspoon chilli flakes

Salt and pepper

30 g (1 oz) mixed seeds

1 bag salad leaves

Sweet Chilli Dressing

2 tbsp oil

1 teaspoon honey

1 tbsp cider vinegar

½ clove garlic, crushed

½ teaspoon chopped chilli

Salt and black pepper to taste

Mix all the ingredients together and leave to marinate for at least an hour but preferably overnight.

Keeps for weeks in a jar.

1. Cut the peel and pith away from the grapefruit, then cut out the segments, dropping them into a bowl as you go.

2. Squeeze the juice into a separate smaller bowl.

3. Peel, stone and slice the avocado. Make sure you don't lose the flesh close to the skin – it is the highest in nutrients.

4. Add to the segments along with the prawns.

5. To make the chilli dressing, whisk together the rapeseed oil, grapefruit juice, garlic and chilli flakes.

6. Check for seasoning, add a little salt and pepper to taste.

7. Put on to salad leaves on plates, sprinkle with the seeds and drizzle with the sweet chilli dressing to serve.

 Copyright © 2016 Conscious Cooking

 Copyright © 2016 Conscious Cooking

Warm coronation
CHICKEN SALAD

Makes two servings

200 g (7 oz) (1 cup) chicken fillets or thighs, cut into strips

Salt and pepper

100 g (3.5 oz) (½ cup) chick peas

Handful of fresh mint leaves, chopped

½ a red onion, finely sliced

1 baby gem lettuce

6 cherry tomatoes, halved

¼ cucumber, sliced in to half moons

1 stick celery, chopped

2 tbsp chopped walnuts

Dressing

2 tbsp natural yogurt

2 teaspoons curry powder

½ clove of garlic, crushed

Squeeze of lemon juice

2 tbsp rapeseed oil

Forget those nasty pots of supermarket Coronation Chicken – this is the real deal – light, tasty and packed with goodness. It's another stunner of a summer dish – perfect packed up for lunchboxes or for weekend picnics and parties with friends.

1. Place the chicken fillets or thighs between two sheets of cling film, season with salt and pepper and give a couple of bashes with a rolling pin to make into a consistent size.

2. Mix all the dressing ingredients together to a thick, just pouring consistency.

3. Heat a griddle pan and when hot, griddle the chicken strips for a couple of minutes each side.

4. Meanwhile mix the other ingredients together in a bowl.

5. Pile salad onto the middle of the plates, top with griddled chicken strips and drizzle over the dressing.

 Copyright © 2016 Conscious Cooking

This is another hugely satisfying soup that really does feel like a whole meal in a mug. The coconut milk makes it feel decadently creamy (once again, fear not – coconut milk is packed with good fats and is extremely good for you). Meanwhile the Thai spices are not just warming and tasty, they pack a strong protective punch too (ideal for cough and cold season).

 Copyright © 2016 Conscious Cooking

Thai butternut
SQUASH SOUP

Makes four servings

1 teaspoon coconut oil

1 large red onion, chopped

4 cloves of garlic, chopped

1 inch fresh ginger, peeled & grated

2 sticks lemon grass, chopped

1 teaspoon vegetable bouillon (Marigold is my preferred brand)

1 teaspoon ground coriander

½ teaspoon chopped chillis

1 medium butternut squash, chopped

1 can chopped tomatoes

1 can coconut milk

Lots of freshly ground black pepper

A squeeze of fresh lime

1. Place a heavy bottomed pan on a medium high heat and melt the coconut oil.

2. Add the onion, garlic, ginger and lemon grass and sweat for two or three minutes until the onions begin to soften but not brown.

3. Add the bouillon powder, spices, butternut squash and chopped tomatoes, reduce the heat and simmer for two or three minutes.

4. Add the coconut milk and allow to gently simmer for about 15-20 minutes.

5. Blend using a stick blender or carefully transfer to a table blender and blend until smooth.

6. Return to the pan and check seasoning and add black pepper and a squeeze of fresh lemon juice.

 Copyright © 2016 Conscious Cooking

We serve this soup on many of our retreats but it's never greeted with such delight as on our Sugar Detox. Almost all the food on this retreat is green and so the sunshine colour of this zingy soup is a lovely change to the eyes and the palate! But don't save it for detox – it's a great lunch dish for any time.

 Copyright © 2016 Conscious Cooking

Roasted Yellow
PEPPER SOUP

Makes four servings

4-5 yellow peppers

2 leeks, topped, tailed and washed

2 carrots, chopped

2 cloves garlic, crushed

4 tbsp olive oil

1 medium onion, finely chopped

2 stalks celery, finely chopped

1.2 litres (2 pints) good quality chicken or vegetable stock (home-made if possible)

2 tbsp fresh thyme, chopped

1 bay leaf

Salt and freshly ground black pepper

Additional olive oil to garnish

1. Cut the top and base from each of the yellow peppers, remove the seeds and then cut into thin strips.

2. Cut the leeks into strips the same size as the peppers.

3. Place the leeks, carrots and peppers in a roasting dish and sprinkle with the garlic.

4. Drizzle two tablespoons of olive oil over the top, season with salt and freshly ground black pepper and place in a medium oven for 40-45 minutes until nicely roasted and soft.

5. Heat two tablespoons of olive oil in a large casserole or saucepan and sauté the onion and celery for five minutes until softened but not browned.

6. Add the leeks and most of the peppers (reserve a few for garnishing), the stock, thyme and bay leaf and simmer for 30 minutes or so until the potatoes are nice and soft.

7. Place the soup in a blender and whiz until smooth.

8. Adjust the seasoning (adding a good grind of black pepper) and serve in bowls, garnished with a little of the reserved roasted peppers and a drizzle of olive oil.

   Copyright © 2016 Conscious Cooking

 Copyright © 2016 Conscious Cooking

Tomato and
CHICKPEA SOUP

Makes four servings

1 teaspoon olive oil

1 onion, chopped

4 stalks celery

1 ltr (1.75 pint) vegetable stock

800 g (28 oz) (4 cups) can chopped tomatoes

1 yellow/orange pepper

1 can chickpeas, drained

2 medium carrots, peeled and chopped

1. In a large saucepan heat oil over a medium heat.

2. Add onion to pan and cook for 3 minutes until softened.

3. Pour stock and tomatoes into pan, bring to a simmer, add the veggies and half the chickpeas.

4. Cover, cook for 20 minutes, stirring occasionally.

5. Blend to a smooth consistency and return to the pot, add the remaining chickpeas.

6. Remove lid and cook for a further 15 minutes.

 Copyright © 2016 Conscious Cooking

 Copyright © 2016 Conscious Cooking

Parsnip and
APPLE SOUP

Makes four servings

4-5 yellow peppers

2 leeks, topped, tailed and washed

2 carrots, chopped

2 cloves garlic, crushed

4 tbsp olive oil

1 medium onion, finely chopped

2 stalks celery, finely chopped

1.2 litres (2 pints) good quality chicken or vegetable stock (home-made if possible)

2 tbsp fresh thyme, chopped

1 bay leaf

Salt and freshly ground black pepper

Additional olive oil to garnish

1. Cut the top and base from each of the yellow peppers, remove the seeds and then cut into thin strips.

2. Cut the leeks into strips the same size as the peppers.

3. Place the leeks, carrots and peppers in a roasting dish and sprinkle with the garlic.

4. Drizzle two tablespoons of olive oil over the top, season with salt and freshly ground black pepper and place in a medium oven for 40-45 minutes until nicely roasted and soft.

5. Heat two tablespoons of olive oil in a large casserole or saucepan and sauté the onion and celery for five minutes until softened but not browned.

6. Add the leeks and most of the peppers (reserve a few for garnishing), the stock, thyme and bay leaf and simmer for 30 minutes or so until the potatoes are nice and soft.

7. Place the soup in a blender and whiz until smooth.

8. Adjust the seasoning (adding a good grind of black pepper) and serve in bowls, garnished with a little of the reserved roasted peppers and a drizzle of olive oil.

 Copyright © 2016 Conscious Cooking

This super simple lunch dish has been a staple on our retreats since the very first one.

The great thing is that even though this serves six people it keeps really well in the fridge for two or three days so is perfect to take to work with salads.

Be sure to use fresh courgettes or the water content might be too high and you will end up with a wet frittata that does not set well.

 Copyright © 2016 Conscious Cooking

Courgette and pea
FRITTATA

Makes six servings

1 teaspoon rapeseed oil

1 small onion, chopped

3 courgettes, grated

175 g (6 oz) (1 ¼ cups) frozen peas, defrosted

2 teaspoons fresh tarragon, chopped

2 tbsp fresh parsley, chopped

8 eggs, beaten

Salt and pepper

25 g (1 oz) (¼ cup) parmesan cheese, grated

1. Heat the oil and gently fry the onion until soft but not brown.

2. Add the courgettes and cook on a low/medium heat for five minutes.

3. Add the peas and herbs to the mix.

4. Season the eggs with salt and pepper and pour over the vegetables.

5. Reduce the heat and cook for three or four minutes.

6. Scatter cheese on top then pop under a medium grill for five minutes until the top is solid and golden brown.

7. Serve with a green salad.

Copyright © 2016 Conscious Cooking

This is a great side dish but can easily be turned into a veggie main by adding a tbsp of crème fraîche to the sauce, then sprinkling with chopped almonds and serving with wholegrain basmati rice or on a piece of toasted sourdough bread.

Copyright © 2016 Conscious Cooking

Mushroom RAGOUT

Makes four servings

1 large onion

3 tbsp rapeseed oil

200 g (7 oz) (2 cups) chestnut mushrooms

100 g (3.5 oz) (1 cup) large flat mushrooms

100 g (3.5 oz) (1 cup) mixed mushrooms

2 garlic cloves

60 ml (2 oz) red wine

Salt and pepper

1. Soften the onion in the rapeseed oil for five minutes.

2. Add the mushrooms and garlic, cook for three minutes.

3. Add the wine and cook until almost evaporated – around eight minutes.

4. Season with salt and pepper

 Copyright © 2016 Conscious Cooking

Make vegetables the stars of the dish. You can mix and match the veggies you use to fill the parcels to suit your taste and according to what you have in the fridge. This really is a moveable feast.

These veggie parcels also make a good accompaniment to a meat dish like a griddled chicken breast.

 Copyright © 2016 Conscious Cooking

Veggie
PARCELS

Makes four servings

2 large aubergines, sliced lengthways into
6 pieces

2 tbsp grapeseed oil

8 asparagus spears

1 carrot, chopped into long batons

4 broccoli spears (sprouting broccoli)

1 ball mozzarella, chopped

4 sundried tomatoes, chopped

Handful fresh basil leaves

30 g (1 oz) (¼ cup) pine nuts, toasted

Cocktail sticks to serve

1. Brush aubergine slices with oil and cook under a medium grill for two to three minutes each side until golden. Do not allow them to get too dark.

2. Cover with foil and leave to one side.

3. Blanch the other vegetables in gently boiling water for two to three minutes.

4. Drain and put to one side.

5. In a large bowl mix the mozzarella, tomato, basil and pine nuts.

6. Spread the cheesy mix along each aubergine roll.

7. Place vegetables on top and roll up, secure with a cocktail stick.

8. Place in the fridge on a baking tray to chill and firm up for at least 20 minutes.

9. Put in the oven for about 20 minutes until cooked through.

10. Serve with a green salad.

 Copyright © 2016 Conscious Cooking

Make this dish in advance
and eat it cold or warm,
but it is also delicious hot,
Add some fresh lemon juice
for a zesty flavour if you
want to.

 Copyright © 2016 Conscious Cooking

Quinoa with roasted
VEGETABLES

Makes two servings

1 small red onion, coarsely chopped

1 red, yellow or orange bell pepper, coarsely chopped

1 small courgette, coarsely chopped

2 cloves garlic, thinly sliced

1 tbps olive oil

150g (1 cup) cherry tomatoes

1 cup quinoa

1 tsp low salt vegetable bouillon (broth) powder

2 cups boiling water

50g (2 heaped tbps) pumpkin seeds

50g (2 heaped tbps) flaked almonds

Large handful fresh spinach leaves

Preheat the oven to 400°F (200 ° C)

1. Place the onion, peppers, courgette and garlic in a roasting pan, drizzle with olive oil and stir to coat. Roast for 30 - 40 minutes.

2. Meanwhile, place the quinoa and broth powder in a pot and add the boiling water. Bring to the boil, cover and reduce the heat. Simmer for about ten minutes until the liquid is absorbed and the grains are fluffy. Set aside until the vegetables are cooked.

3. Five minutes before the vegetables are done, spread the pumpkin seeds in a dry frying pan and gently toast.

4. Stir the roasted vegetables into the quinoa, sprinkle the toasted pumpkin seeds and flaked almonds on top.

   Copyright © 2016 Conscious Cooking

You know how it is when you have a saucy dish for supper, you naturally want something to help soak up the sauce and so it has become almost instinctive for us to reach for pasta, rice or other grains. However, especially in the evening, you don't want the heaviness of these carbs. So when we have a saucy dish on retreat we often serve it with "Caulirice" (sometimes I call it "Caulicouscous"). Often our retreaters have no idea that it isn't actually a grain as it is so tasty and light. It puts a whole new slant on cauliflower, trust me!

Anyhow, try it for yourself. It really couldn't be easier to prepare but the key it have a fresh firm cauliflower; not something that has been lurking at the back of the fridge all week.

 Copyright © 2016 Conscious Cooking

CAULIRICE

Makes four servings

Half head of cauliflower

40g mixed seeds

Salt & freshly ground black pepper

1. First grate your cauliflower and set to one side until about five minutes before you are ready to eat.

2. Take a large sauté or frying pan and place on a high heat. Tip in the grated cauliflower and seeds into the dry pan and simply warm it through for about two to three minutes. Keep stirring so that the cauliflower doesn't stick to the bottom of the pan. Season with a little salt and pepper and that is it. Done. Yes, it's that simple.

3. A nice variation is to add in half a head of grated fresh raw broccoli - this gives a vibrant green colour while at the same time upping your veggie intake for the day. It's a great way to get kids to eat their greens too.

 Copyright © 2016 Conscious Cooking

Courgetini or Courgette
RIBBONS

If you haven't already tried raw courgette "spaghetti" that is all about to change. This is, quite simply, the perfect alternative to pasta. I tried many, many, many times to perfect recipes I read on the Internet but somehow always seemed to end up with mush. This way is fool-proof, I promise. I use it all the time on retreat when I can be catering for up to ten people and there's not a mushy noodle in sight!

The key is to use fresh firm courgettes. The older they are, the higher the water content and, consequently, the less good the noodle.

Makes four servings

4 large, very firm courgettes

1. Either spirilize your courgettes or use a peeler to create full length ribbons.

2. Then place the ribbons in a colander over a bowl and leave for up to an hour to dry out a little.

3. About ten minutes before you need them, form your ribbons into nests on a lined baking tray and pop into a warm oven, about 140 is good. Allow to warm up gently.

4. Using a fish slice, place a nest on each plate and top with your sauce or dressing of choice.

Marvelous MAINS

As I've said before, it's entirely up to you to decide which time of day works best for you to eat your main meal. It will largely depend on your daily schedule, your activity levels and your own metabolism.

Some people find that that they cannot digest a large meal in the evening and that it leaves them with indigestion, reflux or IBS symptoms – or just that it lays heavy on the stomach before bed. Others like to sit down with family at the end of the day and relax over a long meal together.

The choice is yours, so learn to listen to what your body needs. Notice how you feel after you eat and for a few hours afterwards. Some days it may suit you to eat a larger meal in the middle of the day while other times you may want to treat yourself to a slap up dinner...there is no right or wrong, there is only choice and balance.

 Copyright © 2016 Conscious Cooking

This is a robust Greek dish, full of gutsy flavours. If you have a slow cooker, you could let this cook even more slowly, as the Greeks do. It makes a warming nourishing supper on cold nights and is also a great meal for sharing with friends round the kitchen table.

 Copyright © 2016 Conscious Cooking

Beef
STIFADO

Makes four servings

Heat oven to 180F°/350°C/gas mark 4

1 k (2.2 lb) (4 cups) beef shin or braising steak

Juice of 1 lemon

A little flour

4 tbsp grapeseed oil

0.5 ltr (1 pint) red wine

3 tbsp red wine vinegar

1 teaspoon sugar

1 teaspoon salt

1 teaspoon oregano

½ teaspoon chilli flakes

½ teaspoon all spice

4 cloves

2 bay leaves

1 kg (2.2 lb) (10 cups) baby onions

2 cloves garlic

700g (1 lb) (3 cups) passata

1. Put the braised meat, wine, vinegar, sugar and spices in a pan. Bring to a gentle simmer.

2. Peel onions and fry until golden brown. Add the garlic and passata and stir through.

3. Add the passata mix to the beef and bring to a gentle simmer.

4. Cover and transfer to the oven for one hour.

5. Serve with a green salad in the summer or with 'caulirice' in the winter.

Note: To help break down the connective tissue of the beef marinate it overnight in the lemon juice. This add a lightness in terms of texture and flavour that really complements the dish and makes it easier on your digestive system.

 Copyright © 2016 Conscious Cooking

People tend to shy away from duck, thinking it's a difficult meat to cook properly. The truth could not be more different. This way of cooking duck is so simple that it is perfect every time.

 Copyright © 2016 Conscious Cooking

Duck breast with lime and HONEY

Makes two servings

Preheat the oven to 200°C/400°F/gas mark 6

2 medium duck breasts

salt and pepper

2 shallots, sliced

100 ml (3.5 fl oz) vegetable stock

¼ glass white wine

2 limes – 2 zested, 1 juiced

1 teaspoon honey

140 g (5 oz) (3/4 cup) wholegrain basmati rice to serve.

1. Heat a frying pan on a high heat.

2. When the pan is hot sear the breasts in the dry pan, skin side first, for one minute each side. You are looking to render down the fat from the duck, which is why you want a hot dry pan.

3. Place on a baking tray, season and cook in the oven for ten minutes, then remove and cover with foil to rest for up to another ten minutes.

4. Discard at least half of the duck fat from your pan leaving just a little and now fry the shallots in the oily pan until soft.

5. Add the stock and the wine to a pan and bring to the boil.

6. When at a steady boil add the zest, juice and honey.

7. Simmer for three to four minutes.

8. Season.

9. Slice the duck breast and top with the sauce.

10. Serve with wholegrain basmati rice.

   Copyright © 2016 Conscious Cooking

This dish originally started as "Marrakesh Not Fried Chicken". It was my take on a famous takeaway chicken dish but made with spices I had bought in the souk on my travels to Marrakesh. But it's not such a catchy title, so now it's simply Moroccan Spiced Chicken.

Think soft and juicy chicken surrounded by spicy savoury crunch and you have the idea...but oven baked and so light and clean. The spicing is very subtle but, if you have fussy eaters, you could easily reduce the quantities by half and it will still be tasty.

Ras el Hanout is a traditional Moroccan spice mix, now readily available from supermarkets and health stores.

 Copyright © 2016 Conscious Cooking

Moroccan Spiced
CHICKEN

Makes four servings

4 organic chicken breasts

50g sesame seeds

1 tsp ground cumin

1 tsp ground coriander

½ tsp smoked paprika

½ tsp Ras el Hanout (optional)

1 lemon, juice and zest

1 tbsp tahini

1 tbsp rapeseed or rice bran oil

Salt & fresh ground black pepper

Preheat your oven to 180° degrees

1. First slice your chicken breast into thick long strips. I like to cut mine into thirds as a rule of thumb but it depends on how big your bird is.

2. Next take the sesame seeds and spices and mix them together. You can either do this in a large freezer bag (saves on the washing up) or in a bowl.

3. Next mix together your wet ingredients - the lemon, tahini and oil - and liberally coat your chicken strips in the mixture.

4. Now toss your chicken strips in the spicy seed mixture. At this point you can wrap them up and leave in the fridge for a couple of hours or up to one day as this will really allow the flavours to infuse.

5. When you are ready to cook simply toss the chicken strips onto a preheated baking tray and cook for 25 – 30 mins. Check your chicken after about 15 mins and turn to ensure they are browning evenly.

6. I like to serve this chicken dish with Caulicouscous (see Caulirice in Lunch section)

 Copyright © 2016 Conscious Cooking

We don't often cook lamb on Retreat as it is not to everyone's taste, but I love it. Using a cheaper cut of meat here not only keeps the cost down but actually makes it taste better.

 Copyright © 2016 Conscious Cooking

Lamb with herbs
AND LEMON

Makes two servings

1 tbsp grapeseed oil

25 g (1 oz) butter

2 lamb chump steaks (175 g (6 oz) (1.25 cups) each

1 medium onion, chopped

2-3 cloves of garlic, chopped

1 level teaspoon dried oregano/herbs de Provence

250 g (9 oz) (1 ½ cups) carrots, diced

2 tbsp sun dried tomato paste

1 level teaspoon caster sugar

1 lemon – rind thinly pared and chopped, the juice squeezed

200 ml (7 fl oz) vegetable stock

Salt and pepper

20 g (3/4 oz) (3/4 cup) pack of flat leaf parsley

150 g (5 oz) (1.5 cups) wholemeal pappardelle pasta to serve, or make your own courgette ribbon pasta (see recipe in SIDES)

1. Heat the oil and butter in a pan, add the lamb and brown.

2. Transfer to a plate.

3. Add the chopped onion to the pan, lower the heat and soften (approximately ten minutes).

4. Stir in the garlic, oregano and carrot and cook for two minutes.

5. Combine tomato paste, sugar, lemon juice and stock.

6. Return the lamb to the pan, pour over the above mix.

7. Bring to a simmer, season, cover and cook for 40 minutes.

8. Prepare the pasta.

9. Mix the lemon rind and parsley and sprinkle over the lamb just before serving.

 Copyright © 2016 Conscious Cooking

These are fabulous whether you cook them on the barbecue or on the hob. These koftas can be made up days ahead of time and they also freeze really well – so it's worth making up a batch.

 Copyright © 2016 Conscious Cooking

Lamb KOFTAS

Makes four servings

1 onion, grated

450 g (1 lb) (2 cups) minced lamb

1 teaspoon coriander seeds

1 teaspoon cumin seeds

1 teaspoon chilli powder

2 tbsp flat leaf parsley

2 tbsp pine nuts

1 teaspoon dried oregano

2 tbsp grapeseed oil

½ cucumber, grated

2 tbsp mint, chopped

150 ml (5 fl oz) (10 tbsp) natural yogurt

Salt and pepper

1. Mix the onion and lamb together.

2. Use a pestle and mortar to blend the spices and add them to the lamb, along with the chilli powder.

3. Chop the parsley, pine nuts and oregano, add to the bowl and mix well.

4. Take a small handful of the mixture and push on to a small wooden skewer.

5. Squash it down to make a sausage shape. You should get 20.

6. Heat a little oil in a pan and fry for three to four minutes each side.

7. Mix the cucumber, mint, yogurt and salt and pepper and serve with the koftas.

 Copyright © 2016 Conscious Cooking

CAPONATA

I have been making caponata for decades now. I know this dish isn't a looker but it is super simple to rustle up and tastes fantastic. A word of warning – this dish can be addictive! I have been known to have this almost every night for a week.

These days I freeze it in individual portions as soon as it is cool.

Makes six servings

1 tbsp grapeseed oil

1 aubergine, cubed

1 red onion, cut into chunks

2 courgettes, cut into chunks

3 mixed peppers, cubed

5 ripe tomatoes, cut into chunks

1 tin of tomatoes, chopped

200 ml (7 fl oz) vegetable stock

1 teaspoon smoked paprika

½ teaspoon ground cumin

¼ teaspoon cayenne pepper

Juice and zest of 1 lemon

Salt and pepper

2 rye crackers

50 g (1.5 oz) (1 tbsp) cooked quinoa

50 g (1.5 oz) mixed seeds

Handful of chopped parsley

30 g (1 oz) (¼ cup) parmesan, grated

1. In a large pot or pan, heat the oil and fry the aubergine and onions until soft but not brown.

2. Add the courgettes, peppers and fresh tomatoes. Cook for a few minutes.

3. Add the tin of tomatoes, stock and spices. Stir well, cover and cook on a gentle simmer for about an hour, checking and stirring regularly.

4. Prepare the topping by crushing the crackers and mixing with the chopped parsley and cheese.

5. Add the lemon juice and zest to the caponata and season with salt and pepper.

6. Spoon the mixture into an oven proof dish, sprinkle with the topping and then place under a hot grill until golden.

7. You can freeze the caponata at the stage where you add the lemon juice and zest and then top and grill once defrosted.

 Copyright © 2016 Conscious Cooking

 Copyright © 2016 Conscious Cooking

Lemon Chicken
STIR FRY

Let me start with a confession – I don't usually like stir fry! What I really don't like is that it is usually either swimming in sauce, or flat and bland. This recipe allows you to make the dish as spicy and as saucy as you like and it's not remotely soggy.

It takes under 15 minutes from start to finish – I promise!

Makes two servings

Juice of 1 lemon

1 tbsp soy sauce

1 small red chilli, deseeded and finely chopped

2 inches of fresh ginger, grated

1 teaspoon Coconut Oil

200 g (7 oz) (1 cup) skinless chicken breast, cut into strips

4 spring onions, sliced

100 g (3.5 oz) (3/4 cup) broccoli florets

50 g (2 oz) (½ cup) sugar snap peas

1 yellow or orange pepper, cut into slices

2 garlic cloves, crushed

2 tbsp hot water

40g (1 ½ oz) (1/4 cup) whole grain basmati rice to serve

½ teaspoon sesame seeds

1. Mix the lemon juice, soy sauce, chopped chilli and ginger.

2. Heat half the oil in a wok or large frying pan.

3. Stir-fry the chicken for about six to seven minutes until cooked through.

4. Set to one side and cover with foil.

5. In the same pan stir-fry the vegetables in the remaining oil for two minutes.

6. Stir in the lemon sauce and add the chicken.

7. Add as much of the water as you desire to create your desired amount of sauce.

8. Serve with the rice and sprinkle with the sesame seeds.

Sea Bass with FENNEL SALAD

Makes two servings

2 sea bass fillets

Rapeseed oil

1 large orange

1 fennel bulb

½ red onion

1 tbsp white wine vinegar

40 g (1 ½ oz) (1/3 cup) black olives

1 teaspoon whole grain mustard

Handful of dill

Salt and black pepper

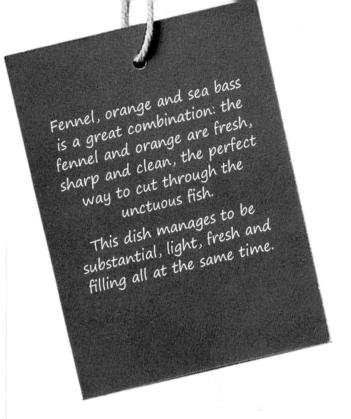

Fennel, orange and sea bass is a great combination: the fennel and orange are fresh, sharp and clean, the perfect way to cut through the unctuous fish.
This dish manages to be substantial, light, fresh and filling all at the same time.

1. Rinse the fish and dry with kitchen paper. Brush with the rapeseed oil and season.

2. Cut the orange in half. Zest and juice one half and set to one side. Peel and thinly slice the remaining half.

3. Thinly slice the fennel and onion.

4. Panfry the fish fillets in a tablespoon of rapeseed oil, skin side down first, for one or two minutes on each side until golden.

5. To make the dressing, add one tablespoon of rapeseed oil to the orange juice and mustard and a sprinkle of chopped dill.

6. Serve on a plate, topping each fillet with alternate slices of orange, fennel and onion.

7. Drizzle with the dressing and top with chopped dill.

   Copyright © 2016 Conscious Cooking

Few things can say "home" like a tasty satisfying fish pie. The addition of the fresh tarragon is key here as it really lifts the flavours. Meanwhile the crème fraîche makes the sauce light yet still feeling indulgent. This is everything a fish pie should be.

 Copyright © 2016 Conscious Cooking

Special
FISH PIE

Makes four servings

Heat oven to 190°C/370°F/gas mark 5

350 g (12 oz) (1 ¾ cups) haddock or cod fillet, skinned

1 tbsp cornflour

115 g (4 oz) (½ cup) cooked peeled prawns

75 g (3 oz) (½ cup) sweetcorn

75 g (3 oz) (½ cup) frozen peas

2 boiled eggs, peeled and quartered

150 ml (5 fl oz) milk
(you can use nut or soya milk)

150 g (5 oz) (1 ½ cups) half fat crème fraîche

1 large handful fresh tarragon

Salt and pepper

75 g (3 oz) (1 ¼ cups) fresh wholemeal/Rye breadcrumbs

25 g (1 oz) (1 tbsp) sesame seeds

40 g (1.5 oz) (⅓ cup) grated Pecorino Romano cheese

Selection of fresh vegetables to serve

1. Cut the fish into bite-size pieces and toss in the cornflour to coat evenly.

2. Place the fish, prawns, sweetcorn and peas in the ovenproof dish.

3. Beat together the milk, crème fraiche, tarragon and seasonings, then pour into the dish.

4. Top with quartered boiled eggs.

5. Mix together the breadcrumbs, sesame seeds and grated cheese, then spoon over the top of the dish.

6. Bake for 30 minutes until golden brown and serve fresh with hot vegetables.

A note about low fat/half fat diary options. Often when manufactures take out the fat, they replace it with sugar, sweeteners, flavourings and thickening agents – to try to replicate the flavour and texture that fat gives. Make sure to read the label of the produce you choose and ensure that it is simply a strained product; nothing added, just fat taken away.

    Copyright © 2016 Conscious Cooking

 Copyright © 2016 Conscious Cooking

Baked Portobello Mushroom
RISOTTO

I like to serve this risotto on a bed of rocket, topped with a sprinkling of Pecorino Romano cheese.

Makes two servings

2 large portobello mushrooms

1 small onion, finely chopped

1 garlic clove, finely chopped

3 chestnut mushrooms, chopped

1 tbsp rapeseed oil

Pinch of salt

80 g (2.8 oz) packet (10 tbsp) of barley*

500 ml (17 fl oz) good quality stock

25 g (1 oz) (1.5 tbsp) parmesan cheese, grated

Handful fresh parsley

1 bay leaf

1. Heat oven to 170°C/325°F/gas mark 3.

2. Remove the stalks from the portobello mushrooms. Place the mushrooms onto a baking tray.

3. Finely chop the onion and garlic – the finer you are able to make your chopping, the better your risotto will be.

4. Heat a tablespoon of rapeseed oil in a pan and sweat down the garlic and onion.

5. Add a pinch of salt.

6. Keep the heat medium, you do not want the onion colour. It will take at least five minutes of stirring to make the onions sweet and juicy.

7. Add the barley. Now add the stock in three batches and stir – each time the liquid is absorbed, add the next batch.

8. Add in the chopped

> * Do try to get hold of pot barley. This is barley still with its fibre jacket intact. It adds fibre and slows down the sugar absorption of the starches.

   Copyright © 2016 Conscious Cooking

Mickey D's Pepper
CRUSTED FISH

You know how men sometimes master one or two dishes in the kitchen and then they become their "go to" special meals? This is one of those dishes. My friend's husband, Michael, mastered this dish shortly after they married. It was so good I just had to pinch it! Thank you Michael, it's still a winner every time.

Makes two servings

1 heaped tbsp whole mixed peppercorns (coarsely crushed)

1 heaped tbsp plain flour, seasoned with a little salt (you can use gluten free flour)

2 x 150 g portions (7 oz) of fresh cod fillets (or cod tails)

1 tbsp rapeseed oil

Vinaigrette:

1 clove garlic, peeled

2 level teaspoons coarse ground mustard

Grated rind and juice of 2 limes

4 tbsp olive oil

Salt and freshly ground black pepper

Fresh coriander leaves, chopped

New potatoes and green beans to serve

1. Mix together the crushed peppercorns and seasoned flour.

2. Remove the skin from the fish. Wipe with kitchen paper then coat with the peppercorn mixture, pressing well on both sides.

3. Set aside while preparing the vinaigrette.

4. Crush the garlic into a bowl and stir in the mustard, lime rind and juice, four tablespoons of olive oil, seasoning and coriander.

5. Heat a tablespoon of rapeseed oil in a large frying pan.

6. When hot, add the fish and fry for three minutes on each side, until crisp and golden.

7. Keeping the same heat, pour the vinaigrette around the fish and maintain heat to reduce. This will take only a few minutes. Be warned there may be a bit of spluttering that goes on once the vinaigrette hits the pan. This is natural but be ready to stand back.

8. Serve with new potatoes and green beans.

    Copyright © 2016 Conscious Cooking

Medieval
SPICED PORK

If you thought recipes were bland back in medieval times, think again! Our ancestors used a variety of spices and herbs, not only to flavour their dishes, but to help preserve them. Honey was commonly used as a sweetener, before the advent of sugar – far healthier! This recipe isn't entirely authentic but who's going to quibble when it tastes this good?

Makes six servings

Preheat oven to 150°C/300°F/gas mark 2
900 g (2 lb) (4 cups) pork shoulder steaks
2¾ tbsp rapeseed oil
1 large onion, chopped
2 garlic cloves, crushed
1 level tbsp plain flour
1 level teaspoon ground ginger, coriander and paprika
½ teaspoon ground cinnamon
300 ml (10 fl oz) red wine
Juice of ½ an orange and 1 thin strip of peel
1 bulb fennel, trimmed and cut through root
100g (4 oz) (1 cup) dried apricots, cut in half
1 tbsp runny honey
1 sprig fresh rosemary
Salt and pepper
Couscous and a green salad to serve

1. Trim meat and cut into large chunks.

2. Heat two tablespoons of oil and quickly sear the meat. Remove to a casserole dish.

3. Fry the onion in the remaining oil until soft.

4. Add the garlic and cook for one minute.

5. Add the flour and spices and cook for one minute.

6. Add the wine, orange juice, orange peel, fennel, apricots, honey and rosemary.

7. Stir and bring to the boil.

8. Cook for one and a half hours covered, stirring halfway.

9. Serve with couscous and a green salad.

    Copyright © 2016 Conscious Cooking

Moroccan Vegetable Tagine &
COUSCOUS

This is a big favourite with our retreaters...not only on retreat itself but when they return home armed with a folder of recipes from their retreat. It's so easy to make and it freezes beautifully - so it's perfect for batch cooking.

Makes four servings

45 ml (1.5 fl oz) vegetable stock

1 green pepper, seeded and sliced

2 medium courgettes, sliced

2 medium carrots

2 celery sticks, sliced

1 aubergine, chopped

400 g (14 oz) (2 cups) chopped tomatoes

100 g (3.5 oz) (¾ cup) chopped dates

5 g (1 teaspoon) chilli powder

1 tbsp ground cumin

1 teaspoon cinnamon

400 g (14 oz) (2 cups) drained chickpeas

Black pepper

2 tbsp chopped fresh mint

120 g (4 oz) (½ cup) couscous

20 g (0.75 oz) ((1/8 cup) raisins

2 tbsp pomegranate seeds

Mint to garnish

1. Heat the stock in a large flameproof casserole until boiling.

2. Add the sliced pepper, courgettes, carrot and celery. Stir over a high heat for two to three minutes until the vegetables are beginning to soften.

3. Add the aubergine, tomatoes, dates, chilli powder, mint, cumin and cinnamon.

4. Add the chickpeas and bring to the boil.

5. Reduce the heat, cover the casserole and simmer for 30 minutes or until all the vegetables are tender.

6. Season with black pepper and serve hot, garnished with mint leaves.

7. Add couscous and raisins together in a bowl and prepare as per packet instructions.

8. Before serving scatter pomegranate seeds on top of couscous.

9. Garnish with mint.

 Copyright © 2016 Conscious Cooking

 Copyright © 2016 Conscious Cooking

Cassoulet is a classic cold weather peasant dish, solid, rib-sticking hearty food. But the traditional dish is seriously heavy and tough on the arteries! By combining the sausage and duck breast together into dumplings this indulgent dish becomes almost lean.

This is an impressive dish to serve at a dinner party.

 Copyright © 2016 Conscious Cooking

Toulouse Sausage
CASSAOULET

Makes four servings

3 Toulouse sausages

1 small duck breast

2 cloves garlic

2 brown onions, sliced

40 g (1.5 oz) (¼ cup) bacon lardons

1 stick celery, chopped

1 large carrot

1 glass white wine

200 ml (7 fl oz) chicken stock

400 g (14 oz) (2 cups) chopped tomatoes

Herbs de Provence

1 leek, sliced

400 g (14 oz) (2 cups) haricot beans

Zest of an orange

TO MAKE THE DUMPLINGS:

1. Remove the skin from the sausage, and cut up one duck breast, one clove of garlic and half an onion roughly chopped.

2. Blitz all the ingredients until well combined and shape into small meatballs. Cover and allow to chill while you make up the cassoulet.

TO MAKE THE CASSOULET:

3. Fry the bacon lardons in a hot pot to release the fats then add the remaining sliced onion and garlic. Soften but do not brown.

4. Add the celery and carrot and cook for a few minutes.

5. Add the wine, stock and tomatoes and herbs, cover and allow to cook for about 15 minutes.

6. Then add the leek and beans and cover again for a further ten minutes.

7. Meanwhile, heat a large frying pan until very hot, then dry fry your meatballs until browned all over. You do not need to use any oil as the fat from the sausages will do this for you.

8. Add the meatballs and orange zest to the cassoulet and turn the heat down very low and allow to all mix and meld together for about five minutes.

   Copyright © 2016 Conscious Cooking

This spicy curry is a life-saver on a cold Autumnal evening when you fancy something warming, filling and easy to eat. Don't be tempted to reach for that jar of curry sauce — yes, it's easy but it is packed with added sugar and salt.

Instead make up a batch of this simple yet delicious curry and keep a stash in the freezer for a quick supper dish.

 Copyright © 2016 Conscious Cooking

Spiced Yellow
PEA CURRY

Makes four servings

250 g (9 oz) (1 ¼ cup) yellow split peas

1 teaspoon bouillon

2 tbsp rapeseed oil

20 g (3/4 oz) (1¼ tbsp) butter

3 brown onions, chopped

3 garlic cloves, chopped

1 tbsp grated ginger

1 teaspoon cardamom pods

1 teaspoon turmeric

250 g (9 oz) (2.5 cups) baby spinach

Handful fresh basil leaves

25gms bulgur wheat per person to serve

1. Gently simmer the peas in ½ litre of water with bouillon for about 40 minutes.

2. Meanwhile, in another pan, heat the oil and butter and gently fry the onions until they soften – don't allow them to brown.

3. Add the garlic and ginger and cook for a further five minutes.

4. Add the spices and cook for a further five minutes on a very low heat.

5. Drain the peas when they are soft but still al dente.

6. Reserve the stock.

7. Add the peas to the onion and a glug of the cooking stock.

8. Cover and cook on a low heat for 20 to 30 minutes.

9. You may need to add a little more cooking stock through the cooking to stop the dish from becoming dry.

10. Just before serving, stir in the baby spinach and fresh basil.

11. Serve with bulgur wheat.

 Copyright © 2016 Conscious Cooking

SNACKS

Snack wisely,
but do snack every day.

We suggest that everyone should have at least one snack per day. Usually this would be in the afternoon to bridge that long gap between lunch and supper. But depending on your schedule and activity levels you may need to add in up to two further snacks. Remember, don't go more than four hours between meals – if you know you will have a wait before your next meal, do have a small protein-based snack.

 Copyright © 2016 Conscious Cooking

DATE BALLS

Many shop-bought protein bars and balls can actually be very high in added sugars... yes, even the natural ones. They are also pretty expensive. So, make your own! Truly, they are so simple to make (providing you have a blender or mixer). The other benefit is that you can tailor them to your own personal taste. I'm going to share two of my recipes that always go down a storm on our retreats.

Makes eight balls.

250 g (9 oz) (1.5 cups) pitted dates
160 g (5 oz) (1 ⅓ cups) hazel nuts
100 g (3 oz) (1 cup) ground almonds
½ teaspoon cinnamon
1 tbsp raw organic cocoa

1. Place the dates and hazelnuts in a bowl, cover with boiling water and set to one side for at least 30 minutes.

2. Drain the water and place all ingredients in a blender.

3. Blitz to a thick paste.

4. Mould into eight balls, using your hands.

5. Chill and serve.

   Copyright © 2016 Conscious Cooking

Nut Butter
POWER BALLS

This is another great power ball recipe. Unlike sugary snacks, these won't give you a blood sugar spike (and its inevitable accompanying slump). Rather they will let you power through. They're great to take on hikes and cycles, or to add to lunchboxes for an afternoon snack at work. They're also great post-workout as the protein hit will help repair muscle. Win, win, win!

Makes about 18 balls

100 g (3.5 oz) (⅔ cup) pecans

75 g (2.5 oz) (½ cup) raisins

1 tbsp ground flaxseed

1 tbsp cocoa powder

50 g (1.5 oz) (½ cup) desiccated coconut

2 tbsp peanut butter

Blitz, roll, chill, enjoy!

1. These little beauties will keep in an air tight container in the fridge for a couple of weeks...if you can make them last that long! .

Trail MIX

This makes one serving, but it is a great idea to increase the quantities and make up about half a dozen little baggies. These keep for ages and you can store them in your handbag, your drawer at work or even the glove compartment of the car so you always have a healthy snack to hand when you really need one. We often send our retreaters out on hikes with these – they make a great snack when energy levels are flagging.

3 Brazil nuts

4 almonds

4 walnut halves

1 dried apricot

1 date

Pinch of mixed seeds

Pinch of raisins or sultanas

1. Mix and bag up – you're ready to go!

 Copyright © 2016 Conscious Cooking

This hummus will keep in the fridge for about three or four days.

My top tip is to make up a batch of plain hummus and then each day you can add the additional flavours, according to your taste. This keeps it interesting.

I often use this hummus in place of butter for sandwiches so I am increasing the protein content of the meal while at the same time adding in more flavour to perhaps an otherwise boring old sandwich. A spoonful also makes a great topping for an otherwise plain salad.

 Copyright © 2016 Conscious Cooking

Healthy
HUMMUS

This makes 12 x two tbsp servings.

425 g (15 oz) (1.5 cups) chickpeas

1 tbsp olive oil

2 tbsp tahini

½ teaspoon salt

½ teaspoon ground cumin

¼ cup lemon juice

¼ cup water

Freshly ground black pepper

2 large cloves garlic (or to taste)

1. You can add your own flavours as well – chilli flakes, roasted peppers, paprika or fresh coriander.

2. Rinse chickpeas very well to remove excess salt.

3. Place all items in a food processor and whirl away until it is a smooth paste.

4. Serve with 80 g (2.75 oz) (½ cup) mixed vegetable crudités for the perfect snack.

 Copyright © 2016 Conscious Cooking

Date and Organic
OAT BARS

I'm going to share a little secret with you here...I never make the flapjacks on retreat. My partner in the Body Retreat, Julie Brealy, is the baker on our team and I would never dream of stepping on her baking toes ⏺

Many shop-bought flapjacks are laden with sugars, both refined and natural. So if you choose these as a snack when you're out and about choose wisely: there is probably less sugar in a chocolate bar than in many of the "health" bars available. Our flapjacks use a little honey, stoned dates and apple juice to sweeten.

Makes sixteen servings

Heat oven to 180°C/356°F/160° fan/gas mark 4

200 g (7 oz) (1 ¼ cups) stoned dates

2 tbsp unsweetened apple juice

4 tbsp of honey

100 ml (0.1 ltr) rapeseed oil

200 g (7 oz) (2 cups) of organic oats

1 tbsp pumpkin seeds

1 tbsp sunflower seeds

1 tbsp chia seeds

1. Lightly grease an 18 cm (7 inch) square tin.

2. Place the dates in a small saucepan with two tablespoons of water, bring to the boil and simmer for four minutes until soft and paste-like.

3. Place the lemon juice, honey and oil in a pan and heat gently until melted, add the remaining ingredients, including the date paste, and mix well.

4. Press into the tin, smoothing the surface and bake for 25 minutes until golden.

5. Remove from the oven and cut into 16 bars;

 Copyright © 2016 Conscious Cooking

Date and Walnut
FLAPJACKS

You can never have too many recipes for flapjacks in my book! I love the taste and texture the walnuts give to this alternative recipe. Once again, this recipe relies on honey and dates as its natural sweeteners. Obviously these are still sugars but the protein in the seeds and nuts prevents your blood sugar spiking – they just provide a nice sustained boost of energy.

Makes 16 servings

Heat oven to 180°C/356°F/160° fan/gas mark 4

200 g (7oz) (1 ¼ cups) stoned dates

Juice of ½ lemon

4 tbsp honey

150 ml (5 fl oz) rapeseed oil or vegetable butter

200 g (7 oz) (2 cups) organic oats

1 tbsp pumpkin seeds

1 tbsp sunflower seeds

40 g (1.4 oz) (¼ cup) walnuts

1. Place the dates in a small saucepan with two tablespoons of water, bring to the boil and simmer for four minutes until soft and paste-like.

2. Place the lemon juice, honey and butter in a pan and heat gently until melted.

3. Add the remaining ingredients, including the date paste, and mix well.

4. Press into the tin smoothing the surface and bake for 25 minutes until golden.

5. Remove from the oven and cut into 16 bars.

6. Leave to cool in the tin.

   Copyright © 2016 Conscious Cooking

This juice is a great way to get more greens into your diet. Even better – it tastes amazing (try it and see!). You could also pop this into the freezer for 30 mins to an hour and serve it as a refreshing sorbet.

132   Copyright © 2016 Conscious Cooking

Power JUICE

Makes two servings

1 mango, peeled and stoned
1 cucumber
50 g (1.5 oz) (½ cup) spinach
1 avocado
75 ml (2.5 fl oz) apple juice

1. Put all the ingredients into a blender and whiz to a drinking consistency.

 Copyright © 2016 Conscious Cooking

Apple and Celery
SANDWICH

We serve these sandwiches all the time on Retreat and while at first they don't sound that appealing, there is something really moreish and satisfying about them. Of course there is no bread involved - instead we use apple slices or celery sticks to sandwich together nut butter. Yup, it's that simple.

Trust me – you are going to love this snack.

Makes one serving

Half an apple, sliced

1 teaspoon nut butter

or

1 stick celery (topped & tailed)

1 teaspoon nut butter

1. Just a note on nut butter... You can choose any nut you like – gone are the days when it was just peanut on offer. Try a variety – from cashew through almond to hazelnut. They are all delicious. But do make sure that the nut butter you buy is just that – 100 percent nuts creamed into butter. Many of the brands available on supermarket shelves contain palm oil, sugar, salt and even additives to create a buttery product. Stay away from these poor alternatives. The nut butter we use and recommend on Retreat is Meridian; they offer a wide variety of flavours.

2. Of course, if you have time, you could always make your own

Citrus Green Tea
REFRESHER

When you're not drinking alcohol or standard mixers, you can find that plain water gets a bit boring. This fabulous cordial makes a rather special drink. It's perfect for entertaining, or simply when you want to give yourself a refreshing cool drink that's also packed with antioxidants.

Makes about 500 ml (17 fl oz)

1 organic green tea bag

2 unwaxed lemons

3 unwaxed limes

1 large sprig fresh mint

1 tbsp honey

1. Firstly, place your teabag into a mug or jug and cover with about 300 ml (10 fl oz) freshly boiled water and leave to soak for at least 20 minutes.

2. Meanwhile roughly chop up your lemons and limes, keeping the skins on. Add to a blender, food processor or, if you have one, a Nutribullet, along with the mint sprig (stalk and all) and then add the honey. Spritz.

3. When it has cooled slightly add the cup of green tea to the lemon and lime mix and give a few pulses to blend together.

4. Pop this mixture into a fridge for at least an hour to allow the flavours to really develop.

5. Next pass the mixture through a sieve and press to get all the juice from your pulpy mix.

6. Now you have the most delicious cordial that you can top up either with flat or sparkling water and some ice to make a healthy refreshing drink.

7. This cordial will keep covered in the fridge for about a week.

   Copyright © 2016 Conscious Cooking

Sweet
TREATS

At the right size and in the right proportion to your daily nutrient intake there is no reason why you cannot enjoy a sweet treat if that works for you.

If you find yourself eating more of the puddings and treats than the serving size suggests or find yourself craving more sweet stuff afterwards then it might be an idea to cut this from your daily diet for up to two weeks to allow your appetite to recalibrate. Stick to the serving size and these little treats really are just a mouthful of loveliness

 Copyright © 2016 Conscious Cooking

Citrus Yogurt
JELLY FOOL

This is a super simple little dessert that is a hit with kids big and small. Yes, I'm using commercially bought jelly....not the sugar free stuff but the full fat version. You could use agar or gelatine sheets but then the pudding becomes complicated and, let's be honest, complicated recipes are the ones we never make. As we've said before, if you're eating clean for 80 percent of your diet, the odd jelly (offset as it is here with the yoghurt and milk for protein) won't hurt.

Makes up to six servings

4 large oranges

1 large lemon

1 pack orange jelly

300 g (10 oz) (1.2 cup) natural yogurt

2 tbsp milk

1. Zest the oranges

2. Squeeze the juice from the oranges and lemon.

3. Mix the orange zest with the juice (keep just a little zest back for decoration)

4. Measure out 150 ml (5 fl oz) of the juice mix and add the jelly cubes. Heat on the stove for two to three minutes and stir until dissolved.

5. Make up to 300 ml (10 fl oz) by adding the remaining juice. Leave to cool for about two hours.

6. Reserving three tablespoons of the yogurt, whisk the remaining yogurt into the cooled jelly mix.

7. Pour in to four or six glasses and allow to set in the fridge.

8. Mix the remaining three tablespoons of yogurt into the milk and pour on top of each jelly before serving and sprinkle with the retained zest for a little shot of colour.

 Copyright © 2016 Conscious Cooking

There are many many dairy-free, sugar-free chocolate mousse recipes around but I couldn't resist adding my own take on this classic. What I really like about this recipe is how versatile it is. Once you have mastered the chocolate base then you can go wild with flavours to suit your personal taste: hot chilli, violet extract, cardamom – the world is your chocolate oyster, so to speak. On retreat I keep it pretty simple and I tend to make mint chocolate mousse.

 Copyright © 2016 Conscious Cooking

Chocolate
MOUSSE

Makes four servings

1 large very ripe avocado

25 g (3.5 tbsp) cocoa powder

25 ml almond milk

1 tsp honey

1 tsp vanilla extract

OPTIONAL ADDED FLAVOURS:

Orange extract and orange zest

Mint extract

Coffee extract

1. Add all the ingredients in a blender or mixer and pulse until smooth.

2. You may need to add a little more milk to create the right soft smooth mousse texture, but go gently.

3. Taste and add any extra flavour you might fancy and then give one final pulse.

4. Transfer to a piping bag and pipe into glasses. If you don't have a piping bag, you can just spoon it out (but give a swirl for added effect!)

5. Chill in the fridge for at least 15 minutes before serving.

6. Try not to leave any longer than four or five hours before serving as the avocado can begin to oxidize and turn your lovely glossy chocolate colour to a darker satin brown. It's not quite as appetising to look at but will still taste seriously good.

 Copyright © 2016 Conscious Cooking

There are few puddings that can beat a crumble. But often the toppings are laden with sugar, wheat and heaps of butter. Of course that's okay for the old indulgence, but this crumble is so delicious and yet so healthy you can make it a part of your regular meal plans. I love this pear and blueberry combo, but you could get creative with your own favourite fruits — apples, rhubarb, peaches, apricots all work a treat

 Copyright © 2016 Conscious Cooking

Fruit
CRUMBLE

Makes four servings

2 medium to large unpeeled pears, cored and coarsely chopped

1 cup fresh or frozen blueberries

Ground ginger and/or ground cinnamon

TOPPING

2 tbsp coconut oil

60 g (2 oz) (⅔ cup) rolled oats

2 heaped tbsp ground almonds

2 tbsp sliced almonds or coarsely chopped nuts, such as pecans, hazelnuts, walnuts or pumpkin seeds or sunflower seeds

1. Place the fruit in a saucepan with a splash of water, cover and cook gently for five minutes or until the fruit softens, stirring from time to time. You can add more water if the fruit starts to stick to the bottom of the pan.

2. Add ginger and/or cinnamon to taste.

3. Meanwhile make the topping. Gently heat the oil in a pan. Stir in the oats and toast gently for a few minutes until they start to crisp.

4. Mix in the ground and sliced almonds (or other nuts and seeds) and remove from the heat.

5. Spoon the stewed fruit into bowls and sprinkle on the topping.

 Copyright © 2016 Conscious Cooking

Rice pudding is often overlooked nowadays as so many of us wince at childhood memories of school puddings. Liberate yourself! This rice pudding can set you free from the sceptre of puddings of the past. It's cooked using whole grain rice and coconut milk which means it's healthy as well as totally delicious.

 Copyright © 2016 Conscious Cooking

Coconut RICE PUDDING

Makes 6 servings

1 can light coconut milk

250 ml (8 fl oz) (1 cup) unsweetened almond milk

185 g (6.5 oz) (1 cup) whole grain rice

1 vanilla pod, opened & scraped

2 tbsp honey

1. To make a really luscious brown rice pudding you have to break the grains up a bit in the food processor so they will release their thickening starches. Put them in a food processor and blitz swiftly.

2. In a large saucepan, bring the coconut milk, milk, rice and honey to a soft boil over medium heat. Reduce heat; cover and simmer for 50-55 minutes or until thick and creamy, stirring occasionally. Remove from the heat.

3. Serve with diced fresh pineapple with toasted coconut and finely grated lime zest, or with your favourite topping - in moderation of course. :)

   Copyright © 2016 Conscious Cooking

Mango and Ginger
PUDDING

This is another great way of sneaking greens into your regular diet. This super speedy little dessert always get a "wow" reaction when I serve it as it tastes soooo much better than it looks. Thank you to Christine Baily at ION (Institute of Optimum Nutrition) who shared the basis of the recipe – of course I couldn't resist adding my own twist. Incidentally, if you have children and despair of getting greens into them, this could be your hidden super-power!

Makes four servings

2 large ripe mangoes

2 large handfuls spinach

1 teaspoon psyllium husks

1 tbsp pea protein powder

½ stem ginger, very finely chopped

Coconut water to blend

1. Place all the ingredients in to a mixer/ blender and pulse until smooth.

2. Transfer to glasses or dishes and chill for at least 15 minutes before serving.

 Copyright © 2016 Conscious Cooking

Rhubarb and Orange
POSSET

I love rhubarb – it's so quintessentially British. This is actually a pretty sophisticated little pudding that would hold its own at any dinner party – or smart picnic. But, again, like all these recipes, it's also healthy enough to eat in moderation as part of your everyday diet.

Makes about 500 ml (17 fl oz)

350 g (12 oz) (3.5 cups) rhubarb, cut into chunks

2 tbsp runny honey

4 tbsp blood orange juice

1 vanilla pod

250 g (9 oz) (1 cup) Quark

100 ml (3.5 fl oz) ½ fat crème fraîche

1 tbsp orange zest

1. Place the rhubarb chunks, honey and two tablespoons of orange juice in a pan and simmer until the rhubarb is gently softened. Scrape out the vanilla pod and add the empty pod to the pan now to allow it to infuse while the rhubarb mix is cooking.

2. Whisk together the Quark, crème fraîche and the remaining orange juice with the scraping of the vanilla pod.

3. Divide the rhubarb mixture between four glasses and top with the creamy mixture.

4. Drizzle a teaspoon of rhubarb juice over the top and scatter with orange zest to finish.

5. Chill for at least 30 minutes before serving.

   Copyright © 2016 Conscious Cooking

Beyond Conscioius
COOKING

This is, first and foremost, a recipe book. We wanted to keep it simple, so you're not overloaded with information. Just by making the changes suggested here, shifting the way you eat and what you eat, you will notice huge beneficial changes. However, as you will have realised, we're not just about food at The Body Retreat. If you come on one of our retreats you will certainly enjoy good food – but that's just the start of it.

You will also learn about behavioural tricks to cement your healthy lifestyle – simple, effective strategies to live the best life you possibly can. We will also ease you into exercise and make sure you have plenty of rest and relaxation? Why, because in an ideal world, you look beyond the kitchen, putting healthy, self-loving behaviour into your entire life.

By eating well, you have taken the first big step. Let's just touch lightly on how to increase those benefits with a few extra guidelines.

Exercise
FOR LIFE

Can you be healthy without exercise? Not really. The health benefits of regular exercise and physical activity are hard to ignore, heart health, mental health, bone density, immunity from illness and disease and even your sex life are all improved by regular physical activity. We should all be active during our day to day lives; we are biologically designed to be active beings. However these days very few of us have physical jobs; most of us sit behind a desk for long periods of time and this sedentary lifestyle is literally killing us.

At The Body Retreat we differentiate between exercise and activity.

Activity is simply being more active in your daily life, taking the stairs, strolling to the shop rather than make a short drive, walking the dog. Our bodies quickly become accustomed to these activities and they soon become health maintenance not health improvement.

By contrast, when you exercise with intent, there should be sweat and there should be heavier breathing. You are pushing yourself. This helps you to both shed unnecessary weight and increase strength and flexibility.

Choose something that you enjoy – that really is the key to consistency. Join a class: the choice is huge these days – so everyone can find something they enjoy. A lot of women come on our retreats, try out different activities and are amazed to find they enjoy the most surprising things. Hefting a kettlebell might really rock your boat – or you might fall head over heels with Zumba, or Pilates, or yoga, or circuits, or Boxercise. If you don't try it, you will never know!

Getting a PT is wonderful, of course, as he or she can create a programme tailor-made for you – and also, you can't wimp out when someone is watching. Can't afford that? Buddy up with a friend and motivate one another. Create a home gym space – you don't even need a lot of kit, just a pair of decent trainers. You can use your body weight for simple routines, and then use the great outdoors as your gym – walk, run, cycle, swim – whatever works for you.

    Copyright © 2016 Conscious Cooking

It doesn't matter what you do, just do it! Just remember, if you aren't sweating and out of puff, you are simply being active. That's great, it's a good start, but you won't be burning fat or improving your fitness in any meaningful way.

If you have been sedentary for a long time then start by building up your daily activity levels to the point where you are comfortably active for at least 15-20 minutes every day. Then start to consider what exercise you might enjoy. If you have any health issues or concerns do please speak with your GP or other health professional before embarking on any course of activity or exercise.

R&R

When was the last time that you made time for yourself? I mean made time ...not found time. Almost all the women who join us at The Body Retreat have become very good at neglecting their own R&R. They are very good at looking after everyone else, but not so good at putting their own needs on the To Do List. Sound familiar?

It's important to know that real strength and growth actually come not from the effort of exercise but from the rest and recuperation that follows. This is the time when the muscles repair and build, when the mind calms and clears and the experiences of life are processed. R & R isn't a "nice to have" ...it's a "need to have".

One question I ask on retreat is this: "If you were given an extra 30 minutes a week, what would you do with it?" The only catch is that you must spend the time only on yourself. What would you do? Have a lie-in, take a bubble bath, treat yourself to a shoulder massage, read a book? What would you do with an extra 30 minutes a week? There are 10,080 minutes in every week and carving out just 30 of those for yourself alone sends a very powerful message that you are worth it, that you are a good person who deserves to have something for yourself. It tells your subconscious that you are committed to your overall wellbeing. So I challenge you to make 30 minutes every week and spend it doing something or doing nothing, whatever works for you. You'll be surprised how in just a few weeks you start to notice improvements in your feelings of health and wellbeing

Conscious CONCLUSION

We really hope you've enjoyed this book. Don't just leave it sitting on the shelf – get into the kitchen and get cooking. So many people seem to think that just having the book is enough!

Even by taking small steps – even eating clean and consciously for just a few days a week, you will start to notice huge improvements in your health. Your body knows the truth and you will find that, if you start paying attention to how you feel, you will learn what suits your body and what doesn't.

What we eat affects our mood just as much as it affects our body, so expect to feel lighter in mind as well as body when you follow these recipes. Conscious eating is a bit of a mind diet.

If you find you fall by the wayside, don't beat yourself up. Remember every day is a fresh start. In fact, every hour, every minute, every moment is a fresh start. So just brush yourself down, be kind to yourself, and promise yourself that your next meal will be mindful, conscious and good for you in mind, body and spirit.

Do let us know how you get on with the recipes. You can find us on Facebook (thebodyretreat) and Twitter (@bodyretreatUK) or you can get in touch via our website. We love to talk healthy eating! Tell us which your favourite recipes are. Tell us how you have adapted or tweaked them. Tell us any that maybe don't work for you, and why. We're always learning, always adapting, always (hopefully) improving.

And, of course, if you would like a more immersive experience of Conscious Cooking & Eating, do come on one of our retreats – we would absolutely love to meet you.

Take care. We wish you good health, happiness and many many memorable meals!

Juls and Julie

 Copyright © 2016 Conscious Cooking

RESOURCES

http://www.thebodyretreat.co.uk/the-body-retreat-meal-planners/

SHOPPING LIST

GREENS

Other Veg

Baby spinach

Avocado

Rocket

Bell peppers

Broccoli

Carrots

Spring onions

Celery

Watercress

Cucumber

Cabbage

Onions (Brown & Red)

Leeks

Sweet potato

COURGETTE

Aubergine

Fresh Fruits

Parsnips

Orange

Tomato

Ruby grapefruit

Mushrooms

Lemons

Fresh ginger

Limes

Pomegranate

Pineapple

Mango

Blueberries

Apples

NUTS & SEEDS

Nut & Seed Butters

Almonds

Peanut butter

Brazils

Almond/Cashew butter

Cashews

Tahini

Walnuts

Hazelnuts

Pine nuts

Chia seeds

Pumpkins seeds

BEANS & LENTILS

Sunflower seeds

Sesame seeds

Ground almonds

Ground flaxseed

Desiccated coconut

Unsweetened coconut

Psyllium husks

    Copyright © 2016 Conscious Cooking

DRIED FRUITS
Apricots
Dates
Raisins
Cranberries

DRIED HERBS & SPICES
Dried chilli flakes
Ground cumin
Ground coriander
Ground cinnamon
Mixed spice
Turmeric
Curry powder
Mixed herbs
Oregano
Bay leaves
Cardamom pods
Vanilla pods
Sea salt
Black pepper

FROZEN PRODUCE
Soya beans
Peas
Cannellini beans
Black beans
Chickpeas
Haricot beans
Split yellow peas
Puy lentils

WHOLE GRAINS
Wholegrain basmati rice
Quinoa
Whole jumbo oats

Rye flakes
Buckwheat groats
Pot barley
Pearled spelt

STORE CUPBOARD STAPLES
Coconut milk
Apple cider vinegar
Ground cinnamon
Unsweetened almond milk
Vanilla extract
Honey (raw if possible)
Coconut water
Balsamic vinegar
Soy sauce
Fish sauce
Anchovy fillets
Vegetable bouillion
Canned tomatoes
Canned pineapple in juice
Rapeseed oil
Olive oil
Coconut oil
Black olives
Rye bread
Rye crackers

FRESH PRODUCE
Eggs
Natural yoghurt
Sweetcorn
Prawns
Feta cheese
Parmesan or Pecorino Romano

 Copyright © 2016 Conscious Cooking

About our
RETREATS

We offer a seriously wide range of weight loss, health and fitness holidays and wellness breaks for women who want to reboot their lifestyle and enjoy a healthier future.

The Body Retreat is the perfect balance between spa retreat and health and fitness bootcamp. Our structured courses are carefully designed to ensure the best possible results. All our residential retreat programmes are specially designed to target issues which affect women's health and wellbeing. We will ensure that you leave us fitter, healthier and happier than when you arrived, but just as importantly, you will be equipped with the tools and resources you need to maintain momentum and regain control for life.

THERE IS A BODY RETREAT FOR YOU.

• Weight Loss Retreats are an amazing kickstart which guarantee weight and inch loss, as well as developing a positive, healthy relationship with real food and finding ways to exercise and be active that suit you.

•Stress Re-Set Retreats are specifically designed to tackle the mental, physical and emotional impact of negative stress on the body. This unique programme helps to break out of the vicious "burnout" cycle we can find ourselves in through stress, anxiety, exhaustion and negative emotions. Your body can heal itself in the right environment and with a little help and guidance from our team of experts.

• Our Health & Fitness Holidays are designed for those who are already exercising but who are looking to improve fitness, stamina and strength while at the same time tone up and perhaps shift those last stubborn pounds. This structured fitness holiday is based on the latest fitness protocols and nutritional advice for improving performance along with getting a little bit of sun and a whole lot of the feelgood factor.

the BODY RETREAT

•Sugar Detox Retreats are perfect for those times in your life when you need to revitalize and rid your body and mind of toxins like sugar which can make you feel lethargic and sluggish. If you want to get back your glow on the inside and out while you tame your sugar habit then this is the retreat for you.

• Weekend Retreats are designed to help you get away from it all, stay on track, and support focus on a specific goal or journey, as well as simply enjoying being active and having fun with a group of like- minded women. We have a variety of wellness breaks focusing on Body and Mind so there is a weekend break for everyone's interests.

Find out more on our website: www.thebodyretreat.co.uk
You can also call us on 0203 701 1603 or email info@thebodyretreat.co.uk

 Copyright © 2016 Conscious Cooking

18852055R00086

Printed in Great Britain
by Amazon